# Checking C Programs with lint

# Checking C Programs
# with lint

Ian F. Darwin

O'Reilly & Associates, Inc.
103 Morris Street, Suite A
Sebastopol, CA 95472

**Checking C Programs with lint**
by Ian F. Darwin

**Editor:** Tim O'Reilly

**Printing History:**

| | |
|---|---|
| October 1988: | First Edition. |
| January 1991: | Minor corrections. |

ISBN: 0-937175-30-7

[1/94]

"*lint* is a mixed success. It says exactly what's wrong with [the] program, but it also produces a lot of irrelevant messages ... and it takes some experience to know what to heed and what to ignore. It's worth the effort, though, because *lint* finds some errors that are almost impossible for people to see. It's always worth running *lint* after a long stretch of editing, making sure that you understand each warning that it gives."

– Kernighan & Pike, 1984

"*lint* is a scroll of forgiveness for many sins of programming – read it wisely, and you shall prosper. But fail to read it, and you will hear maniacal laughter."

– Darwin & Collyer, 1985

"Thou shalt run *lint* frequently and study its pronouncements with care, for verily its perception and judgement oft exceed thine."

– Henry Spencer, "The Ten Commandments for C Programmers"

# TABLE OF CONTENTS

# Preface

Scope of This Handbook
Conventions Used in This Handbook

## Scope of This Handbook

This book describes *lint*, a tool developed at the same time as the portable C compiler. *lint* is designed to do error checking on C programs—especially checking for nonportable code.

The book is divided into eight brief chapters and three appendices.

Chapter 1, *Introduction*, gives a brief overview of *lint*—what it is and what it does.

Chapter 2, *Using lint*, gives a few simple examples to get you started.

Chapter 3, *Dealing with lint's Concerns*, discusses some approaches to dealing with what *lint* tells you. This chapter ends with an extensive catalog of the more common complaints that are generated, and hints on exactly what to do about each.

Chapter 4, *Using lint in Detail*, gives more detail on *lint* command line options, and how to use it with *make*.

Chapter 5, *Limits to lint*, introduces some freeware programs that either work with *lint* or solve problems that it does not address.

Chapter 6, *Under the Hood*, contains a cursory look "under the hood" that many readers will want to skip on first inspection.

Chapter 7, *An Evaluation of lint*, gives my personal evaluation of *lint*; Chapter 8, *Future Directions*, gives some ideas on the future of C and *lint*.

Appendix A, *The Ten Commandments for C Programmers*, presents a summary of the ten most important points on style and portability. You don't need to be a UNIX wizard to use this book; on the contrary, it is aimed at the beginning and intermediate C programmer. However, at various places in the book I refer to portability aspects of several variants of the UNIX system.

Appendix B, *A Very Brief History of UNIX*, is therefore an overview of UNIX which introduces the key flavors of the system.

Appendix C, *Supplemental Programs*, contains reference pages for the programs mentioned in Chapter 5. Source code is available via Uunet and other sources.

At the end of the book you will find a bibliography and an index.

## Conventions Used in This Handbook

*Italics* are used for UNIX pathnames, filenames, and commands.

**Boldface** is used for UNIX command options.

`Courier font` is used for anything the user would type verbatim.

# 1

## Introduction

*lint* may be among the most misunderstood — and underestimated—
tools in the UNIX programmer's workbox. *lint* is a most useful tool,
and one that no effective UNIX programmer can do without. *lint*
checks up on programs written in the C language. It verifies a program
or program segments against standard libraries. It checks the code for
common portability errors. It tests the programming against some tried
and true guidelines. *lint*ing your code is a necessary (though not
sufficient) step in writing clean, portable, effective programs.

But *lint* is not perfect. It will not magically salvage bad code. It will
not find all your bugs. It suffers from some false starts, such as the
'irrelevant messages' complained about in the opening quote. One purpose of this book, then, is to tell you "what to heed and what to
ignore." On most versions of UNIX, *lint* does not know how to deal
with *printf*, nor with assignment in conditional contexts. However, just

as a good book may contain a few dull chapters and still be adjudged worthwhile, so may *lint*. As you might skip over outdated political speeches in an otherwise-fast-paced adventure story, it is worthwhile to skip over the irrelevant messages to find the real problems in your code. If your programs are to have a chance of being portable to UNIXes or to other C-capable computers* besides the particular one you use, there are only two choices: use *lint*, or keep your code to yourself. It's unfair to inflict code on the world — whether posting it to USENET or a bulletin board or selling it for profit — without having run some basic portability checking on the code.

Further, *lint* is in the mainstream of one major trend in C compilers, the trend to better and more complete error checking. While it is to be hoped that the C language will never reach the terminal complexity of the **PL/I** language, C continues to grow, and compiler technology grows with it. The earliest C compilers (up to Seventh Edition UNIX, which ran only on PDP-11 computers and was released in 1979) did not warn of most casual coding practices. If you wrote code containing statements that could never be reached, the compiler assumed that you wanted it so. And if you mixed integers with pointers and thought you could get away with it, well, so did everybody else then.

Times have changed: right after that version of the C compiler was finished, people began porting UNIX to all sorts of other computers. And on some of these computers, when you blindly copy an integer variable into a pointer, the results are distressingly unpredictable. Most modern C compilers therefore warn about some glaring errors, such as code that cannot possibly be reached, illegal or dangerous combinations of integer variables with pointers, and others. Two programs from AT&T Bell Laboratories Computer Science Research have been useful allies to those trying to write portable code: *pcc* and *lint*. *pcc* is the portable C compiler; it was written for the early porting efforts, started the trend of adding portability checking into the compiler, and has descendants in the majority of UNIX systems in the field today. *pcc* and *lint* are like twins, conceived in the same mind and born of the same source code. And *lint* is the topic of this book.

---

*It is never going to be the case that everybody in the world is running C on the same kind of CPU. Not the IBM PC. Not the 68000. Not the VAX. Not the 3B. Not the 68020. Not the 80386. Not SPARC. There will always be a variety of CPU types in service, so it will always be necessary to write portable code.

Introduction

Using lint

Dealing with
lint's Concerns

Using lint
in Detail

Limits to lint

Under the Hood

An Evaluation
of lint

Future Directions

# 2

## Using lint

*lint* is invoked in the same manner as any other UNIX command: com-
mandname, options, and filenames. Let's *lint* a simple program, say
*myfile.c* , that has a common error or two.

```
myfunc(s)
char *s;
{
     void a();

     int i, j;
     a("hello");
}
```

Here's an example of running *lint* on a USG UNIX system* and the messages it produces:

```
% lint myfile.c

myfile.c
==============
(6)  warning: i unused in function myfunc
(6)  warning: j unused in function myfunc
warning: argument unused in function:
     (2)   s in myfunc

==============
%
```

On a V7† or Berkeley UNIX system, that example might look like this:

```
% lint myfile.c
myfile.c:
myfile.c(2): warning: argument s unused in function myfunc
myfile.c(6): warning: i unused in function myfunc
myfile.c(6): warning: j unused in function myfunc
%
```

*lint* has several imitators on lesser operating systems. I haven't tried any of these, but any program that claims to be "*lint*-like" should produce the same kind of messages as real *lint* does. The text of the messages may differ, though, so you'll have to do some translation on your own.

There are three error messages here; the Research and Berkeley version presents them somewhat more compactly, although the USG version is more compact in longer printouts. The warnings in this example are self-explanatory; the writer of this function has declared two variables and not used them, and an argument to a function is not used in that function. Most of the messages from *lint* are of this form; they tell

---

*See Appendix B for a short historical overview of UNIX and the origins of the USG and Berkeley variants of UNIX. I use the historically correct but slightly dated term USG (for UNIX Support Group) to refer collectively to UNIX System III, System V, System V Release 2 and System V Release 3.

† On a true museum-piece PDP-11 V7 system, and on some non-UNIX C compilers, you would have to #define or *typedef* the type *void* to be the same as *int*.

what the problem is, and where it lies. A few of its messages, however, are neither this clear nor this easy to understand. We look later in more detail at the most common messages from *lint* and what to do about them.

What do you do with complaints from *lint*? The same as you would do with compiler error messages: correct the error and try again. If you delete the declarations of *i* and *j* and re-*lint* the file, you will get told about the remaining defect(s):

```
% lint myfile.c

myfile.c
==============
warning: argument unused in function:
    (2)  s in myfunc

==============
%
```

Another common error in C is to assign the return value of *getc* to a *char* variable and then compare it with the value EOF. This works on many computers: those for which *char* is sign-extended when promoted to *int\**. Here is *copyfile.c*:

```
/*
 * copyfile(in, out) - simple file copy
 */

#include <stdio.h>

copyfile(fin, fout)
FILE *fin, *fout;
{
     char c;

     while ((c = getc(fin)) != EOF)
          putc(c, fout);
}
```

---

*Even on machines that treat *char* as signed when promoting to wider types, the program can fail: if the data being read by *getc* happens to contain a byte that is all ones (i.e., \377), you will get a false EOF indication, and stop reading prematurely.

This code ran on seven or eight completely different UNIX systems, then whap! It failed catastrophically on another, writing endless bytes of −1 and filling a filesystem. What if its author (a *former* employee of mine) had stopped to run *lint*?

```
copyfile.c
==============
(12)  warning: nonportable character comparison


==============
function returns value which is always ignored
     putc
```

He'd have seen the error right away. Fixing this one is simple: just change c from *char* to *int*, and the program will work on all UNIX systems.

*lint* is like that: it will catch many common errors, and a few not-so-common ones, that can cause annoying failures in ''production'' code. And the complaint about *putc*? I'll come back to that later.

Introduction

Using lint

Dealing with
lint's Concerns

Using lint
in Detail

Limits to lint

Under the Hood

An Evaluation
of lint

Future Directions

# 3

# Dealing with lint's Concerns

Casting: Tell the Compiler You Know Better
LINT COMMENTS—Tell lint You Don't Care
Specific Problems: The Delinting Handbook

The way to "silence" *lint* is to alter your program in response to its suggestions, run the program through *lint* again, and repeat until *lint* is silent. But keep in mind the purpose of using *lint*. *lint* is not some sacrificial altar on which programmers waste their time: the purpose of running *lint* and trying to minimize its output is not to minimize the listing as an end in itself — we're not here to collect merit badges — but to write cleaner, more portable, more effective code. Fortunately, the two goals of silencing *lint* and writing better code seldom conflict; *lint*ing your code usually makes it more readable, more portable, and more maintainable.

## Casting: Tell the Compiler You Know Better

The cast operator has been in the C language longer than most programmers have. But its use remains a mystery to some programmers. It may help to think of a cast as an intermediate variable of the given type; the first book written on the C language says:

> In the construction
>
> *(type-name)* expression
>
> the *expression* is converted to the named type by the [standard conversion rules]. The precise meaning of a cast is in fact as if *expression* were assigned to a variable of the specified type, which is then used in place of the whole construction. For example, the library routine *sqrt* expects a *double* argument, and will produce nonsense if inadvertently handed something else. So if *n* is an integer
>
> ```
> sqrt((double) n)
> ```
>
> converts *n* to *double* before passing it to *sqrt*. [KeR78, p. 42]

The cast is a special form of assignment. So why do you sometimes see an expression cast to type *void* in others' code? Casting to *void* is a time-honored way of telling *lint* that you know that the expression has a value, but that you intentionally disregard it. Consider the common *fprintf(stderr, ...)*. *printf* and its relatives return an error indication if the *printf* fails. But if writing on *stderr* fails, what can you do about it? You cannot write an error message on *stderr*, since you've just learned that *stderr* is broken. And there is no other place you can write an error message with reasonable expectations of having a person read it. When the going gets this bad, your program should consider suicide, by the *abort*(2) system call. Most programmers just ignore the issue; those who are learned in the ways of *lint* (as we hope you will become by reading this book) cast the result to *void*. So instead of just:

```
fprintf(stderr, "%s: -f argument %s invalid\n",
        progname, optarg);
```

use:

```
(void) fprintf(stderr, "%s: -f argument %s invalid\n",
       progname, optarg);
```

which will not produce a complaint from *lint*.

Storage allocated by *malloc*(3) often needs casting. This function returns a block of characters, but this block is often used to store a structure or union. When you call *malloc* to allocate a structure, *lint* will usually complain that the return value is used inconsistently, or otherwise worry about the incompatibility of the assignment. To cure this, cast the pointer returned from *malloc* to the appropriate struct type*. The value returned by *malloc* is guaranteed to be suitably aligned for conversion to any pointer type, so casting it to ''struct anything *'' is safe.

## /*LINT COMMENTS*/—Tell lint You Don't Care

One interesting problem faced in the design of *lint* was to find a way to add another level of commands to C without breaking existing programs. Many tools and programs, including the C preprocessor *cpp*, the C compiler proper, *cb*, and many others that know something of the syntax of the C language would have had to be modified if the language were changed. The solution chosen was to make *lint* look at comments in the C source, an approach also used in various Pascal compilers for compiler directives. If a particular pattern is found there, *lint* will treat it specially. These comments tell *lint* that you know there is something unusual in the next expression or function, and do not wish to be reminded every time you *lint* the code. There are about half a dozen such special comments in *lint*.

---

*Not only structs, of course. One also sees
```
    x = (int *) malloc (n * sizeof(int)).
```

## /*NOTREACHED*/

The BUGS section of most *lint* manual pages states:

> *exit* (2) and other functions that do not return are not under-
> stood; this causes various lies.

Here is *exitlies.c* :

```
/*
 * get a continue/quit response from the tty, exit if 'q'.
 */

#include <stdio.h>

char
ttyin()
{
        char buf[BUFSIZ];
        FILE *efopen();
        void exit();
        static FILE *tty = NULL;

        if (tty == NULL)
                tty = efopen("/dev/tty", "r");
        if (fgets(buf, BUFSIZ, tty) == NULL || buf[0] == 'q')
                exit(0);
        else
                return buf[0];
}
```

This code will generate a bogus complaint:

```
exitlies.c(20): warning: function ttyin has return(e);\
and return;*
```

A reasonable fix is to add /*NOTREACHED*/ before the closing brace;
this tells *lint* that the programmer believes that this path through the
code can never be reached. For clearly it cannot; we know that *exit*
never returns, and there is certainly no return from a *return,* as long as
the system is intact. Since the *if* guarantees that exactly one of these

---

*The semicolons on this message are part of the C syntax, not part of the English
language sentence structure. Ignore them.

two statements will be executed, it is not possible for this function to fall off the bottom.

A better solution would be to enclose the *exit* call and the /*NOTREACHED*/ in braces, like this:

```
/*
 * get a continue/quit response from the tty, exit if 'q'.
 */

#include <stdio.h>

char
ttyin()
{
      char buf[BUFSIZ];
      FILE *efopen();
      void exit();
      static FILE *tty = NULL;

      if (tty == NULL)
          tty = efopen("/dev/tty", "r");
      if (fgets(buf, BUFSIZ, tty) == NULL || buf[0] == 'q') {
          exit(0);
          /* NOTREACHED */
      }
      else
          return buf[0];
}
```

This form is preferable, since it more clearly connects the unreachability with *exit*, the function that alters the language's ideas of flow control.

## /*ARGSUSED*/ and /*VARARGS*/

Often you write a function in one program and use it in another, but only need part of it. That's where /*ARGSUSED*/ comes in. This tells *lint* that the following function is not to be checked for un-used arguments.

I always advise C programmers to avoid writing functions that require a variable number of arguments the way *printf* does. Most UNIX systems today come with a header file called *<varargs.h>* for the few times you must. There is a similar but not interchangeable header called *<stdarg.h>* in the draft ANSI C standard [dpANS]. Both versions define two macros *va_start* and *va_last* and a name (which may be a macro or an external) called *va_end*.

The *<varargs.h>* facility provides a portable method for writing code that depends on variable-length argument lists. A related facility is the *lint* comment /*VARARGS*/, which doesn't make your code portable, but at least lets *lint* know that you don't care that your variable-length-argument function is non-portable. The comment is taken to mean that only the first *n* arguments are to be checked for consistency; arguments beyond *n* may be missing without generating a warning.

But *printf* and friends continue to cause grief for C programmers. Although *lint* with /*VARARGS2*/ will catch the obvious error of omitting the FILE * argument in a call to *fprintf,* both *lint* and the C compiler are helpless in the face of erroneous data parameters in calls to these functions, and the run time library fares little better. This is a significant problem, since as many as a third or a quarter of the *core* files written on UNIX systems are caused by *printf* or *scanf* with bad arguments.

In the Bell Laboratories experimental Eighth Edition (V8) UNIX, *lint* has two long-awaited options:

> /*PRINTFLIKE*n*/ and /*SCANFLIKE*n*/.

These tell *lint* to check the arguments against the type of expression in the *printf* or *scanf* string that is in argument *n* of the function following the comment. The first *n* arguments are checked as usual. Thus:

```
/* PRINTFLIKE3 */
void
Error(origin, fatality, format, a1, a2)
int origin, fatality;
char *format;
char *a1, *a2;
{
```

is a valid header for a function that takes two flags, a *printf* argument string, and up to two additional *printf* arguments. In the call:

```
if (fp == NULL)
    Error(E_FATAL, E_SYSTEM,
    "cannot read control file '%s'", fname);
```

the first three arguments to *Error* will be checked normally, and the third argument will be taken as a *printf* string, and remaining arguments checked for validity (i.e., the argument matching the '%s' must be of type *char\**).

**Caveat:** The Eighth Edition has not been, and never will be, released commercially, and *this option is not generally available.* One hopes that AT&T will soon incorporate this feature in the System V version of *lint.* Since larger segments of V8 than this (streams, RFS, and the filesystem switch) have made it into SVR3, there is hope. Towards the end of the book we'll see a program to check *printf*–like functions for the vast majority of programmers who do not have have access to V8 *lint.*

# /\*LINTLIBRARY\*/

The *lint* comments relating to function arguments must precede the definition of the function; putting them before an external declaration of the function does not buy you anything. In case you're not familiar with this distinction, a *definition* is where you allocate the storage (or define the function) and assign its type. For example, here are the definitions of an integer variable *x* and an integer-returning function *f*:

```
int x;
int f(y)
{
    return y*2;
}
```

A *declaration* is where you refer to the type of something that's defined elsewhere. Here are declarations for the variable and function defined above:

```
extern int x;
extern int f();
```

There can be many (non-conflicting) *declarations* for a variable or function within a program, but there can be only one *definition.*

The manual entry for *lint* says that /*LINTLIBRARY*/

> at the beginning of a file shuts off complaints about unused
> functions [and function arguments] in this file.

(Only some versions include the text in square brackets.) This does not
say much about its use. It is useful when a header file refers to
numerous external functions, many of which are unused. It is also used
when building a lint library from a series of one-line descriptions of
functions, such as building *llib-ln.lc* from *llib-ln* , the short descriptions
of the standard system library routines. In other contexts the same
effect can be had with the *−u* and *−v* options.

## /*NOSTRICT*/ and /*CANTHAPPEN*/

Almost every Research and Berkeley version of the *lint* manual page I
have seen documents the /*NOSTRICT*/ comment, said to shut off
"strict type checking in the next expression." This option has never
been implemented; it was dropped from USG manual pages.

My 1985 paper on programming style (with Geoffrey Collyer) was enti-
tled "/*CANTHAPPEN*/ or /*NOTREACHED*/ or Real Programs
Dump Core*." It must now be admitted that the /*CANTHAPPEN*/
*lint* comment is totally without substance. No version of *lint* known to
man has yet understood such a comment. It is left in the title to remind
us—and the reader — to check for conditions that we all know "can't
happen." As Collyer wrote in that paper: *Things that you know can't
happen, will.*

**Exercises:**

1. We're about to discuss the particular messages that *lint* produces,
   and what to do about them. First, *lint* a couple of medium-sized
   programs that you have compiled and run, and see how many complaints *lint* generates.

---

*The title was actually printed in the proceedings as "Can't Happen or
/*NOTREACHED*/ or Real Programs Dump Core."

## Specific Problems: The Delinting Handbook

In this section we look at the common messages that *lint* generates, and how to fix the code as a result. *lint* can generate over a hundred* different error messages, and it is not our intention to provide explanations for all of them. We deal here with those that have proven most common, or most important, in practice. In the examples below, "xxx" is replaced in a real instance of the message with some variable or function name from your program, and "#" is replaced by the number of the function argument that is in question.

• *nonportable character comparison*
This is a common portability violation, the result of comparing a *char* variable to a value that will fit in a *char* variable on some architectures and not on others. For example, our previous example *copyfile.c* contains such an error:

```
/*
 * copyfile(in, out) - simple file copy
 */

#include <stdio.h>

copyfile(fin, fout)
FILE *fin, *fout;
{
    char c;

    while ((c = getc(fin)) != EOF)
        putc(c, fout);
}
```

This produces a "non-portable character comparison" message on the line comparing *getc*'s return against EOF. *lint* is right to complain, because EOF has the value "–1", which will fit in a char on some systems, but not on others. You should fix the offending code; here it's as simple as declaring 'c' to be an *int*.

---

\* Not including 'usage' clauses, 'file not found' errors, etc.

• *xxx used but not defined*
The message means what it says; a variable or function is used but is
not defined. Sometimes this is due to coding errors. At other times it
can be caused by errors in a system's *lint* library. If it's a genuine
error, chances are that *cc* or *ld* will find it as an error too. Compile and
load the program. If the compiler and loader are happy, disregard the
*lint* complaint.

• *xxx defined but never used*
The opposite of the previous message. You've defined a variable, but
no part of the program uses it. This is wasteful, and you should eliminate the extra code or variable named *xxx*. But beware of code that is
conditionally compiled with #ifdef; it may just be that your condi-
tionals are nested incorrectly or that you are only checking half the
#ifdef'd code. If you blindly delete *xxx*, you may find yourself
retyping it a few months later when you compile the program with a
different set of definitions and the part of the code that needs *xxx* is
compiled. Look carefully before deleting anything substantial!

One common use of unused strings is to store a copyright notice in the
compiled binary version of a file. The following C program will produce the "defined but never used" message:

```
static char *copyright = "Copyright 1990 Acme Widgets Inc.";
main()
{
      printf("hello world\n");
      return 0;
}
```

The standard way to prevent such text strings from generating *lint* complaints is to #ifdef them out when *lint* is running. *lint* always pre-
defines the C preprocessor variable *lint* (in lower case) for this purpose.
You need only say:

```
#ifndef    lint
static char *copyright = "Copyright 1990 Acme Widgets Inc.";
#endif
```

and the character string will be handled normally by the C compiler,
but be discarded by the C preprocessor when *lint* is running.

A few compilers provide special mechanisms for this purpose. AT&T SVR3 compilers have a #ident directive. It remains to be seen if this directive will catch on in mainstream C. For now use #ifndef lint.

• *struct/union xxx never defined*
A curious anomaly in the C language allows you to declare a pointer to a structure without knowing anything about the contents of the structure. It may just be that the code is passing a structure pointer through from a higher level function to a lower level one. This "pointer passing" works on most machines, but is usually considered bad practice. One legitimate use for this coding practice is "information hiding," in which a structure is blindly passed to a function that is the only routine allowed to access its internal fields. Careful editing of the #include's at the beginning of the code will usually eliminate this message. The program will take fractionally longer to compile, but will be self-contained.

• *possible pointer alignment problem*
Unfortunately, *lint* does not know that some pointers to small objects are aligned well enough to be converted safely to pointers to large objects. The return value of *malloc* is a case in point. lint insists on reminding you that this sort of conversion isn't safe in general. These messages are annoying; you just have to "grin and bear it." You can usually ignore them.

• *variable number of arguments*
There are two reasons why you will get this message: accidental omission or inclusion of function arguments, and attempts to write functions with a variable number of arguments. We've said enough about <*varargs.h*> already. Fix your program: avoid variable arguments, or use <*varargs.h*> to write semi-portable code, or at least use /*VARARGS*/ to confess your sins.

• *argument xxx unused in function*
It's not uncommon to get this message after a long editing session. It means that the named function has an argument *xxx* that is not used inside the function body. Beware of having a local and a global variable with names that are only similar when you thought they were identical, with code in the function that refers to the global variable that it is a copy of; you will get some strange side effects. Code like this breaks when torn off for use as a library function. If this argument

really is unused, *lint* can be silenced by /*ARGSUSED*/ before the definition of the function. The following attempt to silence *lint*, however, is doomed to failure:

```
#ifdef lint
int dummy;
dummy = arg3;
#endif
```

This shuts *lint* up until you build a *lint* library using the source of the library. Then you will get complaints every time you use the *lint* library. Better either to fix the code, or use /*ARGSUSED*/.

• *xxx redefinition hides earlier one*
This code is armed and dangerous; approach with caution! The program has a global variable and a function argument or local variable with exactly the same name. This is not wise. Even if the variable in the function is a copy of the global one, it's safer from a program maintenance standpoint to make them separate. Edit it out carefully: for example, change *index* to *fuindex* or something similar. And do be sure to get *every* occurrence within the function body!''

• *argument (#) used inconsistently*
The writer of this code used different kinds of data as argument '#' to the function in two places. For example:

```
argument(2) function xyz used inconsistently\
(llib-lc(209), myfile.c(34)
```

It's your duty to fix the offending code. Nine times out of ten this represents a simple coding error, as simple as

```
fprintf("hello world\n");
```

*lint* will always catch this error, although neither the C compiler nor the kernel will. On at least two different MC68000-based UNIXes, the above *fprintf* will do nothing (no output, but no core dump) at least some of the time. We were surprised when an old program that had been running for months started to dump core when the size of a library function changed. Perhaps fortunately the *fprintf* had been extraneous, so it had not been missed. That's a case of two bugs cancelling each other out. *lint* would have caught the coding bug immediately, and fixing it would have brought the logic bug to light much more quickly.

- *xxx value declared inconsistently*

*lint* thinks that you have used one function with two conflicting return-value types. Most commonly, one forgets to declare a function that returns a pointer to *char* or structure. Or there may be two different functions with the same name; this is usually bad news for the programmer with a deadline to meet, but it's better to find these errors before you ship the product. Finally, this error may be a bug in the system-provided *lint* library. One UNIX workstation had this problem with *signal;* there is no simple fix. If you are the super-user you may be able to fix the *lint* library, otherwise you suffer. And even if you can fix the *lint* library on your machine, you cannot force the manufacturer to fix it on everybody's, so the program still will not *lint* on an un-fixed version. Manufacturers do not like to be told what to do; if the *lint* library is definitely broken, though, you can submit a bug report and hope that they eventually fix it.

Finally, here's a common example of the kind of niggling little differences that still exist between Berkeley and USG:

```
sprintf value declared inconsistently\
llib-lc(286)  ::  fred.c(237)
```

The return value of *sprintf* is *char* * on V7 and Berkeley UNIX, but *int* on USG systems and in the draft ANSI C standard. Which is correct? Both are, but only one is right for any given UNIX system.

- *xxx returns value which is always ignored*
- *xxx returns value which is sometimes ignored*

The problem is just what the message implies; function *xxx* is returning a value that is not used by the caller. A common programming habit is to ignore the return value from

```
fprintf(stderr, ...
```

As we've seen, if this *printf* fails, the environment is so badly fouled up that you'll likely be unable to get any kind of message to the user. But it's just as well to tell *lint* that you do not care, by casting the *fprintf* return to *void.* When you get **all** the occurrences, *lint* will stop nagging.

A somewhat grubbier approach that will only work on some systems is to cheat a little by declaring the function as being of type *void*; this will work if the function source code is somewhere else and you are using *−u*. But if the function is in another source file that you are *lint*ing at the same time, beware!

A final possibility is that you wrote the function with the thought that the returned value would be useful, but never actually needed it. Then, just define the function type to be *void* and remove the expression from the *return* statement.

• *function xxx has return(e); and return;*
Carelessness, usually. The function writer is at pains to return a value in one place, but leaves the function without returning a value in another path. This will often occur together with one of the previous messages about "returns value which is ignored." If "always ignored", it's pretty safe to remove the return expression. Otherwise, you have a logic bug; fix it. Look for functions that return (say) −1 if some error is detected, but if all goes well finish execution without returning any value. See also the earlier notes on *lint* comment /*NOTREACHED*/.

• *long assignment may lose accuracy* The "may lose accuracy" message occurs when when assigning a *long* value to a variable that is, or might be, shorter.

Collyer's dirge:

> Woe unto you, for all the world is not a VAX!

On VAXes and MC68000 processors, most compilers assign the same precision, the same amount of storage, to *int* as to *long*. But this is far from universal. Many fine UNIXes run on machines like the PDP-11, the 8088, and other architectures on which *int* and *long* are not the same size. All that the C language guarantees about the matter is that *int*s are at least 16 bits wide, and that *long*s are probably at least 32 bits wide, and certainly as wide as *int*s. Try this simple test:

```
if (sizeof(int) == sizeof(long))
      (void) printf("All the world looks like a VAX\n");
else
      (void) printf("I'd better be more careful\n");
```

If you run this test, or code that depends on the same equality, on enough different computers, you will learn to be careful.

And remember that the maximum value you can safely store in a signed *int* is therefore $2^{15}-1$, or 32767. Unsigned *int*s can go twice as high, to 65535. A value of 70,000 has no place in an *int* variable; it will be truncated on some machines. What's worse, the constant 70000 has type *int* on some machines and type *long* on others, so it should never be used as a function argument—use 70000L to be safe. If you mean "a large number," use *long*. You may pay a performance penalty on certain large and allegedly fast but expensive computers with strange C compilers, but your code will be portable.

- *illegal combination of pointer and integer, OP =*
Another in the series of "all the world's not a VAX" messages. This code tries to assign a pointer to an *int*, or vice versa. The most common cause of this error is forgetting to declare that some external function returns a pointer; C doggedly defaults unknown external functions to type *int*. For example:

```
#include <stdio.h>

char *
getuname()
{
     char *p;

     if ((p = getenv("NAME")) == NULL)
          return "(no name)";
     else
          return p;
}
```

*lint* will generate such a complaint on the *getenv* () call, because at this point the compiler has no way of knowing that *getenv* returns a *char* \*. Just add the declaration:

```
char *getenv();
```

after the #include and all will be well; this code will now run on UNIX boxes for which *int*s and pointers are not the same size, as well as on those for which they are. And it will pass *lint* on all systems.

This message can also appear with most any operator in place of "=".
"OP ==" means comparison, "OP Cast" means a cast conversion, etc.
The problem and the solution are the same.

• *value type declared inconsistently*
This message is similar to the preceding, and often appears with it. A
function has been declared as returning two different value types.
Commonly a function has been defaulted to *int*, resulting in a conflict
with its real declaration elsewhere in the code or off in the *lint* library.
Or you have declared a function incorrectly somewhere. Most often
this error can be fixed by declaring the correct type of the function in
the program that uses it. Code that has this error will run on most UNIX
systems, but will compile and fail to work on a machine for which *int*
and pointers are different sizes. The only time it's safe to ignore this
error is for functions of type *void,* such as *exit.*

• *warning: xxx evaluation order undefined*
This message is included here not because it's very common, but
because it can be quite baffling to the novice when she or he first
encounters it. The C language doesn't specify what will result when a
variable is both used and changed within the same expression. For
example, in the following:

```
int i;
char *p, *q;

p[i] = q[i++];
```

the person who writes a C compiler is free to perform the increment of *i*
at any point in the evaluation. Although you might expect that a
modern programming language would guarantee that this be performed
as:

```
fetch q[i] into a temporary variable
increment i
store the temporary variable into p[i]
```

the C language specification says it just isn't so. Code that depends on
a particular order of evaluation here is not portable, so *lint* will warn
you. Simplify the code so the incremented variable isn't also used on
its own in the same statement.

Those are all the common *lint* warnings we're going to look at. As you gain experience with *lint*, you will find more. Try to use your understanding of C, and of the messages presented here, to form a model of how *lint* views the world of C programming.

Introduction

Using lint

Dealing with
lint's Concerns

Using lint
in Detail

Limits to lint

Under the Hood

An Evaluation
of lint

Future Directions

# 4

## Using lint in Detail

Command Line Options
Using lint with make
Roll your own lint Library

## Command Line Options

*lint* has some options that are common with those of the C compiler
command *cc* , and some that are unique to *lint*. *–I* specifies the include
directory. *–D* and *–U* respectively predefine and undefine preprocessor symbols.

Let's look at the remaining command line options in alphabetical order
because there are so many of them.

*–a* controls the reporting of assignments of long values to lesser variables; these assignments are potential portability problems. But does
*–a* turn these warnings on or off? In the development of UNIX System
III, somebody acting in the name of consistency inverted the sense of

several switches. There is thus an astonishing portability flaw between V7-derived systems and USG-derived systems that continues to the present day. On Research-derived systems, –*a* turns **on** the reporting of such assignments; on USG systems it turns it **off.** Several options have this "polarity" problem (see Table 4-2); the only practical solution is to isolate the command line options into a *make* variable such as LINTFLAGS and have two versions, one for V7 and BSD systems and another for USG systems. For an example see the section "Using *lint* with *make*" below.

The –*b* option controls complaints about break statements that cannot possibly be reached. Again, on Research-based UNIX the option enables the reporting, while on USG-based systems it disables it. The V7 manual states:

> This is not the default because, unfortunately, most *lex* and many *yacc* outputs produce dozens of such comments.

Thus it seems that the Research and Berkeley version of *lint* has a better default for –*b,* at least if you are brave enough to *lint* the output of *yacc.*

On some Research/Berkeley versions, the option –*c* is used to check casts of questionable validity. For example:

```
% cat lint -c.c
/* LINTLIBRARY */
kludge(s, i)
char *s;
int i;
{
      s = (char *)i;
      ++*s;
      return;
}

% lint -u lint-c.c
% lint -c -u lint-c.c
lint -c.c(6): warning: illegal combination of pointer\
and integer, op CAST
%
```

As you can see, without –*c*, this program *lint*s cleanly; with –*c*, a warning is generated about the casting of an *int* to a *char* pointer. Such casts are in fact "questionable"; they will work on some computers, and (you guessed it) fail on others.

The option *−h* controls checking of various "heuristic tests". These tests are based on expert programmers' experiences with C, and check for certain kinds of bugs and some practices that are poor style. These checks will find bugs caused by misunderstandings about the precedence of C operators, for example, so you should normally enable these checks. And the test:

```
unsigned int x;
if (x < 0)
    printf("weird\n");
```

can never succeed because unsigned *ints* are always zero or positive, but the C compiler won't tell you that. *lint* will, with the heuristic checking enabled. On Research and Berkeley UNIX versions, *−h* enables the checking; on USG systems it disables the checking.

The next two options control checking of your program against standard libraries. *−n* prevents checking your program against the standard *lint* library (the *lint* library for the C library) and the portable C library. *−p* enables checking your program's portability to other dialects of C. The latter dates from the time when UNIX was used within AT&T to write C code for use on other operating systems like IBM's TSO and Honeywell GCOS. The meaning of *−p* has changed somewhat over the course of time. It now provides a check against a minimal common subset of the C library*. If your program passes *lint* with *−p*, it is likely to do well with any reasonably standard implementation of C. But the contents of the "portable C *lint* library" change periodically; examine the contents of */usr/lib/lint/llib-port* before taking it too seriously. Indeed, some vendors no longer offer the -p option and do not distribute the 'port' library. Instead, more specialized libraries may be included. Here is a listing of Sun's *lint* libraries directory for SunOS 3.0.

---

* The System V Release 2 version of *lint* is reported to back down on some perfectly valid checking—that of *ints* vs. pointers—unless the *−p* option is used. If so, this is a mistake on the part of the developers.

Table 4-1: Sun lint Libraries

| Name | Function |
|------|----------|
| *llib-lc* | standard library |
| *llib-lcgi* | graphics |
| *llib-lcore* | graphics |
| *llib-lcurses* | *curses* terminal library |
| *llib-lm* | math library |
| *llib-lmp* | |
| *llib-lpixrect* | graphics |
| *llib-lsuntool* | graphics |
| *llib-lsunwindow* | graphics |

There are quite a few libraries, many of them for window graphics, which is Sun's forte. But there is no *llib-port* portability library.

Three final options control checking related to arguments and externals. *−u* controls checking of both external variables and external functions that are used and not defined, or are defined but not used. As the manual states, "this option is suitable for running *lint* on a subset of files of a larger program." Thus, if you want to check only one or two files in a directory containing many files from a larger program, use:

```
lint -u main.c file1.c
```

To silence *lint* about unused arguments in functions, use *−v*. Usually unused functions indicate programming errors; you may have just converted one large function into a few smaller ones, and incorrectly referred to a variable that is now global instead of the copy of it that you are passing as an argument. On all systems that I know of, this option suppresses the checking.

Finally, *−x* controls whether variables that are referred to as external, but are not actually used, should be reported. On USG systems and in the SVID, this checking is on by default, and the option disables the checking. On Research and Berkeley systems, use *−x* to enable the reporting. Declaring external variables and then not using them is mildly wasteful—the compiler has to parse the declarations and then winds up discarding them—so you should run this checking periodically.

The *System V Interface Definition* specifies that, effective with SVR2, options *–g* and *–O* of System V *cc* will be accepted to make *lint* look like *cc*, but not affect *lint*'s behaviour. If the *lint* program is written as a shell file (see Chapter 6, *Under the Hood*), it can easily be extended to support this method.

To wrap up, here is a summary of the options that *lint* will accept on the systems we've discussed.

Table 4-2: Lint Options Summary

| | What It Checks | V7 | 4.2BSD | SVR2 | SVID |
|---|---|---|---|---|---|
| –a | long assignments | enable | enable | disable | disable |
| –b | unreached breaks | enable | enable | disable | disable |
| –C | create *lint*lib | n/a | create | n/a | see –o |
| –c | incremental *lint* | – | – | enable | enable |
| –c | check casts | y | y | n/a | n/a |
| –D | same as *cc* | define | define | define | define |
| –g | symbol table (ignored) | – | – | – | – |
| –h | heuristics/style | enable | enable | disable | disable |
| –I | same as *cc* | – | – | – | – |
| –n | standard library | disable | disable | disable | disable |
| –o | create *lint*lib | – | see –C | – | create |
| –O | optimise (ignored) | – | – | – | – |
| –p | portable to non-UNIX | enable | enable | enable | enable |
| –u | unused fns & vars | enable | enable | disable | disable |
| –U | same as *cc* | undefine | undefine | undefine | undefine |
| –v | unused args in fns | enable | enable | disable | disable |
| –x | unused external vars | enable | enable | disable | disable |

## Using lint with make

The standard *Makefile* entry that I use for *lint*ing programs looks like this:

```
LINTFLAGS = -ha # add -ha on V7; remove on USG
LINTLIBS = # add any local lint libraries here

lint: $(SRCS)
        lint $(LINTFLAGS) $(SRCS) $(LINTLIBS)
```

This runs lint for you. What do you do with the *lint* output? You may choose to add the string > $@ to the *make* rule, which will cause the *lint* output to be stuck in a file called *'lint'*. Alternately, if you expect little output, let it print on *stdout*, which normally goes to your terminal (*lint* prints its warnings on *stdout*, not *stderr*—why?). When you need the *lint* output in a file, just redirect it, or say:

```
% make lint | tee lint.out
```

which prints it on your terminal and puts it into a file.

For larger projects, or on a slower system, you may want to do incremental checking. If you are on a recent System V, you can use "incremental *lint*ing" with *lint* −*c*. The SVID states that −*c* causes one ".ln" (*lint* intermediate) file to be produced for each .c source file, and *lint* is then run again without −*c* on all the ".ln" files to list any problems with inter-module references. The SVID also states:

> This scheme works well with *make;* it allows *make* to be used to *lint* only the source files that have been modified since the last time the set of source files was checked with *lint.* [SVID2, p. 354]

Although this scheme was claimed to "work well with *lint*", it is necessary on at least one contemporary version of *make* (SVR2 on an AT&T 3B2), to include explicitly the rules for the ".c to .ln" translation. A *Makefile* for such a system might look like this:

```
SRCS = a.c b.c main.c
OBJS = a.o b.o main.o
LLNS = a.ln b.ln main.ln

prog: $(OBJS)
      cc *.o -o prog

lint: $(LLNS)
      lint *.ln

.SUFFIXES: .c .ln
.c.ln:
      lint -c $<
```

Once you get it working, this method substantially reduces time spent *lint*ing, since each module is only run through *lint* when its source is changed, but you still have the benefit of checking the inter-module references each time. Here is another method for use on non-SVID systems; this method only *lints* the changed modules, and does not check their inter-module references.

```
SRC = main.c scan.c parse.c

lint:      $(SRC)
           lint $(LINTFLAGS) -u $?
           touch lint
lintall:   $(SRC)
           lint $(LINTFLAGS) $(SRC)
```

This will only re-*lint* source files that have changed since the last run, unless you say make lintall. *lintall* will also re-check for inconsistencies between modules, so it's wise to use this make entry periodically.

Berkeley UNIX systems include an additional tool named *error* (1). If this program is available to you, learn to use it. *error* reads as its *input* the error message *output* from the compiler or a compiler-like program* such as *lint*. The program then inserts these error messages

---

\* Here we see another argument for "doing things in a standard way": *any* program whose error reporting is in a form such as:

```
      filename(linenumber): error-text
```

can be used with *error*. According to the man page for error, it knows about the error message formats produced by *make, cc, cpp, ccom, as, ld, lint*, the Berkeley Pascal interpreter *pi* and compiler *pc*, and *f77*.

in place right in the body of your program, marking them with a special comment (in the case of C, /*###), rewriting the source files in place. The file can then be edited again; the ### comments make it easy to find the error messages in context. Usage is as simple as:

```
make lint | error
```

if you have the standard *make* rules described above. *error* is smart enough to toss away extraneous lines, such as the *lint* command that is echoed by *make*.

A session might look like this:

```
% lint -ha a.c
a.c:
a.c(6): warning: j may be used before set
a.c(5): warning: i unused in function a
a defined( a.c(4) ), but never used
% lint -ha a.c | error
1 file contains errors "a.c" (3)

File "a.c" has 3 errors.
     3 of these errors can be inserted into the file.
You touched file(s): "a.c"
% cat a.c
void
a(s)
char *s;
/*####4 [lint] a defined( a.c(4) ), but never used%%%*/
{
/*####5 [lint] warning i unused in function a%%%*/
     int i, j;
/*####6 [lint] warning j may be used before set%%%*/
     *(s+j) = ' ';
}
%
```

**Exercises**

1. Run your favorite program through whatever version of *lint* or similar program you have available. Compare the format of the output to the two examples given. If there are differences, are they useful or useless? Do they help or hinder use of postprocessors such as *error*?

2. Because the format of output was changed between Research and USG systems, *error* cannot be used on USG versions of *lint*. Write a shell file that converts the output from USG *lint* into a form that *error* (1) can process: 'filename(lineno): message'. If you have access to both kinds of systems, take the output from a USG *lint* along with the source program to a Berkeley-derived system and run it through your script and then *error* (1); if you lack access to both, convince yourself logically that your output is in the right form.

3. If you do not have the incremental *lint* option (–c on SVR2), see if you can add it to a copy of your system's *lint* shell script.

## Roll Your Own lint Library

A *lint* library is a description in *lint*'s own terms of the details about a set of C functions. There are two main passes to *lint*, the syntax analysis and the inter-module reference checking. A *lint* library is just the output of running the first pass against all the functions in a C library, saved in a special form on disk that can be read in later when you are *lint*ing a program that uses that library. Just about every C programmer has her own set of personal favorite functions; many keep them in compiled form in a library using *ar*. And most sites doing significant programming develop their own function libraries too. Once you have a private library of C functions, it's easy to make a *lint* library for it. Having done so, you can tell *lint* about the library just as you tell the compiler about a local library.

There is a misconception that one must build a file of one-line descriptions of each routine, as is done for the C library in */usr/lib/lint/llib-lc*. This file contains one-line dummy routines, like:

```
int getopt(ac, av, ol) int ac; char **av, *ol; { return (ac); }
```

But it's not necessary to build this kind of "summary" file to make a *lint* library; they're just there for convenient inspection. Computers get paid to extract relevant information from files; people should not have to do such mundane tasks.

In the case of the C library, there was a good reason. The standard library source is large and is in many subdirectories; running *lint* on all the files at once would be tedious. In the olden days, too, some of the routines were written in assembler, and C interfaces had to be invented. And the source for the *lint* library has to be available online for inspection; it's easier to look in one known file.

But there are two drawbacks to the file of one-liners. It's possible for this file of one-line descriptions to get out of sync with "reality", i.e., the real source code and the documentation (not to mention that those two may disagree!). And global definitions that occur in the real source (such as *optind* and *optarg* in the case of *getopt*) can get lost in the shuffle, resulting in extraneous chatter from *lint*. For a small to medium-sized library, the source of which will be available to the programmers using it, the best approach is usually to run *lint* with some special options on all the library source files at once.

Of course, the techniques for making a *lint* library differ from system to system. On SunOS systems (derived from 4BSD), the code is built into *lint*; to make library *llib-libglyphic.ln* you just say:

```
% lint -Cibglyphic -chnu glyinit.c glyphic.c code.c kpuse.c
glyinit.c:
glyinit.c(65): warning: illegal pointer combination
glyphic.c:
code.c:
code.c(48): warning: illegal combination of pointer and \
        integer, op CAST
kpuse.c:
%
```

As the example shows, you'll also see any errors normally seen in *linting* the functions; this may be another reason the standard library is built from one-line descriptions rather than the real code.

On my personal machine *lint* lacks this option, so I use this shell file, which should work on V7 and many System V systems. The only assumption is that the passes of *lint* are named *lint*1 and *lint*2 and that they're stored in the *lint* directory (see $L in the shell script).

```
:
#! /bin/sh
# mkllib -- make lint library
```

```
PATH=/bin:/usr/bin ; export PATH

H=/tmp/llib$$
L=/usr/lib/lint
O="-C -Dlint -E"

# parse args for validity
set -- `getopt 'abhuvxD:I:U:' $*`
if test $? != 0
then
      echo "usage: $0 [lint opts] libname file.c ..." >&2
      exit 2
fi

# process args: most just pass to lint1
for f
do
      case "$f"
      in
      -a|-b|-h|-u|-v|-x)
            O=$O" $f"
            shift;;
      -[DIU])
            O=$O" $f$2"
            shift; shift;;
      --)
            shift ; break ;;
      esac
done

trap "rm -f $H; exit" 0 1 2 15

lib=$1; shift

>lib$lib.ln              # truncate previous tries
for f               # for each file given
do
      cc $O $f | # lint1 it to make the library
            $L/lint1 -vx -H$H $f >>llib-l$lib.ln
done
```

This concatenates together all the output files from *lint*'s first pass *lint*1. They are binary files with some internal structure. *lint*'s second pass, *lint*2, will read this file to get a description of all the modules and use this information to check the inter-module references, that is, inconsistencies in definition or declaration between one module and another.

The SVID specifies a third way of creating *lint* libraries. Taking a cue from the C compiler, SVID versions of *lint* use *−o* to specify the output file, the output being a *lint* library.

Introduction

Using lint

Dealing with
lint's Concerns

Using lint
in Detail

Limits to lint

Under the Hood

An Evaluation
of lint

Future Directions

# 5

## Limits to lint

printfck
clash and shortc
cchk
check

Now we turn our attention away from using *lint* and examine ways of
going beyond it. Here we discuss common errors that *lint* misses, and
how to catch them. Specifically, we discuss some public domain programs that can be used to extend *lint* or compensate for some of its
deficiencies. Information on how to get sources for these programs is
given in Appendix C.

### printfck

One potential trouble area in the C language is *printf* and its kin. If
you tell *printf* to format something as an *int*, and really pass it a *float*,
the routine that does the formatting has no way of knowing that you've
passed it the wrong kind—and possibly the wrong number—of bytes of

data. Most versions of *lint* do not know about *printf*–like functions. A program named *printfck* by Andries Brouwer of CWI in Amsterdam was posted to the USENET group "net.sources" in April, 1985. The program acts as a front end to *lint*, allowing it to check the correspondence between the format specifications of *printf*–like functions and the number and type of actual arguments. The program prepends the line:

```
#include "pent.h"
```

to each source file, and replaces each call to a *printf*–like function with an expanded form. For example:

```
sprintf(buf, "A %20s%*d", s, m, n);
```

is rewritten as:

```
sprintf(buf, "A %20s%*d", pent_s(s), pent_d(m), pent_d(n));
```

You must either permanently change the source files with *printfck* and leave these function calls in place (they could be eliminated for real compiles with *cpp* macros), or create a temporary copy of each source file.

File *pent.c* is as follows\*:

```
/* LINTLIBRARY */
int         pent_d(d) int d; { return(d); }
int         pent_f(f) float f; { return(f); }
long        pent_DPs) long D; { return(D); }
unsigned long   pent_U(U) unsigned long U; { return(U); }
char        pent_c(c) char c; { return(c); }
char *      pent_s(s) char *s; { return(s); }
```

File *pent.h* is just the *extern* definitions for those functions. Note the effective use of an existing tool: all *printfck* has to do is alter each *printf* call by matching each %x in the format and its corresponding variable y with pent_x(y). The definitions in *pent.c*, and *lint*, do the rest. *lint* can do the checking with:

---

\*I added the /\*LINTLIBRARY\*/ comment to reduce needless chatter from *lint*.

```
lint -options pent.c other_sources ...
```

I tried out the program on a simple test case. Here's the source file:

```
main()
{
    long d = 3;
    float f = 24;

    (void) printf("hello, today is %s, temperature %f\n", d, f);

    exit(0);
}
```

You can see the bug; it's obvious in a program this short.

```
hello, today is ?B(^| OQ^O.X/H, temperature 24.000000
```

But trying to spot one bug like that in a page of *printf*s in a large report writer or an interactive game will convince you of the need for automatic checking. Here's how *printfck* did:

```
% printfck <test.c >ntest.c # make temp copy
% lint pent.c ntest.c # run lint

===============
value type declared inconsistently
    exit          llib-lc(62) :: ntest.c(9)
function argument ( number ) used inconsistently
    pent_s( arg 1 )          pent.c(7) :: ntest.c(7)
%
```

Not bad. It found the error, telling me that line seven of file *ntest* has an inconsistent argument. Remember that this is line six of my original source file; the #include has to be on a separate line because it's a C preprocessor directive, so all the line numbers are off by one. *printfck* would be useful after de*lint*ing a large program; you'd want to get rid of most of the other lint first so that the *pent* messages would stand out clearly.

*printfck* is a good idea, but not a total win because of the amount of work needed to use it. Given a choice between the Eighth Edition UNIX /*PRINTFLIKE*/ and *printfck*, I'd certainly take V8. But until /*PRINTFLIKE*/ makes it into System V, *printfck* will remain a useful addition to the effective UNIX programmer's toolkit.

# clash and shortc

There remain some C compilers that do not use more than seven characters* to differentiate between identifiers. Any high school student can (some with difficulty) compute the astronomical number of variables that seven-character names permit. In my next book I may present some guidelines for choosing variable and function names within this seven-character namespace. But *lint* will not spot variable names that are non-unique in the first seven characters.

Two freeware programs—*clash* and *shortc*—deal with the problem of too-long identifiers. *clash* reports identifiers that are not unique in the first *n* characters (default seven, since that is the length at which most older UNIX C compilers stop comparing). It is quite fast. One problem is that it does not really know either C or the preprocessor very well. For example, it will confuse the *default* keyword in a *switch* statement with a variable named *defaultfam,* and report this as a clash. Also, the program does not know that, on some older systems, *cpp* keywords have flexnames, while C identifiers do not. It is simply being cautious, perhaps more cautious than I. Another problem is that the program remains ignorant about multi-line character strings continued with '\'.

*shortc,* by contrast, tries to hide the problem. It generates a series of C preprocessor #*defines*† to massage readable programs with flexnames into unreadable programs with short names. To be portable, you would have to distribute this set of defines along with the source. *clash* makes sure the identifiers are unique once and for all. As I prefer the *clash* approach, I have not done much with *shortc* except to verify that it works for simple cases.

---

* ANSI C even allows for crufty old operating systems that only allow **six** identifiers for external names and that are not case-sensitive in external names! I'd consider this sort of restriction intolerable (I'd almost rather write my own assembler and loader than have to put up with such a system), but some of you may be stuck with older operating systems that have these limits.

† If your *cpp* also lacks flexnames, you have to massage the #*define* script into a *sed* script.

Neither *clash* nor *shortc* knows enough about C to do 100% of the job. In particular, they don't know that argument names in function definitions don't matter since these are "by definition" local to the function. For example, in the source to the Berkeley mail program (*mailx/Mail*), they find a "false positive" clash:

```
% shortc c*.c
#define printhead Aprinthead
% grep printh !$
grep printh c*.c
cmd1.c:          printhead(mesg);
cmd1.c:          printhead(*ip);
cmd1.c:printhead(mesg)
collect.c:collect(hp, printheaders)
collect.c: if (printheaders) {
%
```

The argument `printheaders` used inside the definition of function `collect` cannot possibly conflict with a global variable or function called `printhead`, but both programs cautiously (or simplistically) report it as a clash. In designing a tool of this type, it is better to have a chance of reporting slightly too much than to ever report too little.

## cchk

*lint* does not catch erroneous use of assignment in what is normally a conditional context:

```
char *
func(a, b)
int  a, b;
{
    extern char *msgs[];

    if (a=b)
        return "equal";
    else
        return msgs[a];
}
```

What was probably meant is:

```
if (a=^=b)
    ...
```

No program can catch this class of "error" without also flagging intentional uses of this syntax, since it's a perfectly valid construct. It's hard to differentiate between legitimate uses and accidental misuses of assignment in a normally-conditional context. But there are two programs that do this and some additional checking on C programs: *cchk*, by Steve Draper *et al*, and *check* by Nick Crossley. Let's run these on the above function. First, *cchk*:

```
$ cchk asscond.c
asscond.c, line 7: *Assignment instead of equals in conditional.
asscond.c: *Summary:
$
```

*cchk* successfully caught the error on line 7. The "Summary:" line is for some other warnings that *cchk* can generate, such as mismatched quotes, nested C comments, etc. *cchk* is a mixed success; the version I have was posted to USENET as "work in progress", and needs some revision before it could be called production-quality code. But it does catch the assignment-in-conditional error. And it can be compiled without *yacc* and *lex*, which are needed for the more ambitious *check* program.

## check

Let's see how *check* fared with the file above:

```
% check asscond.c
asscond.c: assignment in conditional context at or near line 7
%
```

They both caught the same error. The *check* program used a little more CPU time, but it's more general. See the manual pages in Appendix C to see what each program checks for. I like *check*. My only quibble so far—and it's very minor—is that I would have named it *ccheck* since "check" is so vague—does it print checks, balance a checkbook, check whether someone I want to ask out to lunch is logged on, or check the validity of COBOL programs?

**Exercises:**

1. Get a copy of the *printfck* program. The initial version of *printfck* was, as the author described it, "a quick hack" to check some specific source files. To make it more useful, make it read the list of functions to be checked from a file—at present they are defined in the source.

2. Make *printfck* create the temporary output file automatically; be sure you can never clobber an existing file. Should this be done in C code or by wrapping a shell file around the program?

3. There are some minor problems with *printfck*'s interaction with preprocessor directives (e.g., parts of a *printf* statement between #ifdef's or #define's containing quotes). Fix these.

4. Fix *clash* so it can recognize continued strings. Find and fix any other differences between this program and current C language practices.

5. Running *lint*, *clash* or *shortc*, *printfck* and *cchk* or *check* is a lot of work. Write a shell script called *cv* (for C Verify) that does all this checking. Should your run this after every edit, or just after a large editing session, or only when you have an amok program that you can't otherwise debug?

We've looked at several programs for going beyond *lint*. *printfck* checks up on the arguments to *printf*. *clash* and *shortc* let you compile longname programs on an older C compiler that doesn't use all the characters in a name to distinguish names. And *cchk* and *check* check several attributes of programs. One of the exercise suggests ways of combining these checks.

Introduction

Using lint

Dealing with
lint's Concerns

Using lint
in Detail

Limits to lint

Under the Hood

An Evaluation
of lint

Future Directions

# 6

## Under the Hood

This section discusses some internal aspects of *lint*, and can be skipped on first reading. I review the main pieces of the program and show by an example shell script how these pieces can be fitted together.

Fortunately, *lint* is a shell script on most UNIX systems, and is therefore readily visible. To see how *lint* is built on your system, give the command:

```
$ file /bin/lint /usr/bin/lint
```

to look at *lint* in */bin* or */usr/bin*. (One of these locations should work; if not, ask somebody who knows where it is. Hint: try the *which* command if it exists on your system.) You should get something like:

```
/bin/lint: commands text
/usr/bin/lint: can't stat (No such file or directory)
```

which tells you that *lint* exists, is in */bin*, and is a shell script. If you get this far, examine the shell script on your system before you read any further, and see what you can learn about its operation. If you find that *lint* is an "executable," that is, the binary output of a compilation and loading process, read on right away.

I was dissatisfied with the *lint* shell script provided with my system, so I wrote my own:

```
:
#! /bin/sh
# lint -- C program checker

PATH=/bin:/usr/bin:/usr/lib/lint ; export PATH
USAGE="usage: $0 [-abhgnOpuvx][-l lib][-I dir][-Dsym][-Usym] \
        file..."

T=/tmp/lint.$$              # intermediate file
H=/tmp/hlint$$             # header temp file
LL=/usr/lib/lint          # where lint lives
O="-C -Dlint"             # reasonable cpp options
X=
P=unix                    # default library
trap "rm -f $T $H; exit" 1 2 3 15

# parse args for validity
set -- `getopt 'abhl:npuvxD:I:U:' $*`
if test $? != 0
then
      echo $USAGE >&2
      exit 1
fi

# process args
for f
do
      case $f in
      -[IDU]) O="$O $2"; shift;; # CPP options
      -g)   ;;                    # compatability, ignore
      -l)   cat $LL/llib$1$2.ln >>$T; shift;;   # '-l' lintlib
      -n)   P=""   X="$X$1" ;;    # '-n' - no lib check
      -O)   ;;                    # compatability, ignore
      -p)   P="port"  X="$X$1" ;;# '-p' - use port lib
      -*)   X="$X$f" ;;           # other lint parm(s)
```

```
    esac
    shift
done

# Can't pipe to cc or cpp, so not here either;
#      must be >=1 file
case $# in
    0) echo $USAGE >&2; exit 1;;
esac

# process files:
# run thru cpp then lint1, passing filename as arg
for f
do
    case "$f" in
    *.c) (/lib/cpp $O $f | lint1 $X -H$H $f >>$T)2>&1 ;;
    *.ln) cat $f >>$T           # private lintlib
    *)    echo "$0: unknown file $f (must be .c or .ln)" >&2;;
    esac
done

case $P in                      # ? C lib, Port lib, or none.
    unix) cat $LL/llib-lc.ln >>$T ;;
    port) cat $LL/llib-port.ln >>$T ;;
esac

if test -s $H                   # if lint1 did anything, ...
then
    $L/lint2 -T$T $X -H$H       # run lint second pass
fi

rm -f $T $H
```

This parses the options with the standard argument parser *getopt* (1), then runs the source file(s) through the same *cpp* as does the compiler, then through two programs, *lint1* and *lint2* . These correspond to the two passes of the portable C compiler—one to analyze the program, and another to generate the machine-specific instructions that implement the program in your computer.

Introduction

Using lint

Dealing with
lint's Concerns

Using lint
in Detail

Limits to lint

Under the Hood

An Evaluation
of lint

Future Directions

7

# An Evaluation of lint

*lint* is a major tool for measuring your program's portability, and to a lesser extent its correctness. While catching most of the common portability errors, it misses several:

- It does not check *printf* calls to ensure that the format option matches the types of the variables (use *printfck*).

- It does not check variable names that are non-unique in the first seven letters (use *clash* or *shortc*).

- It does not catch accidental assignments in contexts that are normally conditional (use *cchk* or *check*).

Despite these few omissions, *lint* proves itself time and again to be one of the most useful tools available for checking C programs, both yours and others', for portability and correctness. Now that you know how to use it, do so.

Introduction

Using lint

Dealing with
lint's Concerns

Using lint
in Detail

Limits to lint

Under the Hood

An Evaluation
of lint

Future Directions

8

# Future Directions

What does the future hold for C program checking? *lint* will be with us
for at least as long as there are C compilers, certainly until the end of
the century. But the C world is headed in two major directions: ANSI
C and C++.

As we go to press, the long-awaited ANSI C standard is still in ''draft
proposed'' status, but it should receive final official blessing soon.
There are a great number of changes to the language, far too many even
to summarize here. See [KeR88] for a summary, or [dpANS] for all
the details.. Many of the draft Standard's changes are in the direction
of increased error checking. In particular, the proposed ANSI standard
provides for declaration of arguments in function declarations, as does
the C++ language. For example:

```
$ cat eg.ansidef.c
/*
 * a boring function definition
 * with ANSI-style argument declarations.
 */
void
funct(int x, char **as)
{
      int i;

      for (i=0; i<x; i++)
           printf("%s\n", as[i]);
}
$ cat eg.ansiuse.c
/*
 * Main program with ANSI C argument prototypes.
 */
main(int argc, char **argv)
{
      char **data_array;
      int i;
      /* ANSI C external declaration for function: */
      extern int funct(int x, char **as);

      /* load up data_array */
      /* ... */

      /* process it */
      funct(i, data_array);
}
```

We can look forward to the day when all the header files provided with an ANSI C compiler contain argument prototypes. The compiler will then be able to catch and eliminate one major source of run-time problems: incorrect argument lists. And *lint* will be one step closer to obsolescence. But this continues the long tradition of putting more checking into the C compiler. See [Ros84] for some thoughts on C's evolution, as well as the draft ANSI C standard [dpANS] itself.

The C++ language (see [Str86]) is an object-oriented extension of C. It is preferable to many object-oriented systems in that it is a compatible superset of the C language. It provides language mechanisms for automatic storage management and for information hiding, both of which contribute to cleaner, more reliable programming. C++ has been advanced as a replacement for the C language. Although C++ continues to attract a growing cadre of programmers, it's too soon to say how it will fare as a replacement for C. We will also see how much error checking can be automated by extending the language, and whether *lint* has to be rewritten or merely extended for C++. There are apparently no plans for a C++ *lint* at present.

As well, Syntax-Directed Editors (also called Program Synthesizers) have been claimed to prevent or reduce the errors that get into source programs in the first place; these are an obvious area where careful planning of the "templates" used to specify valid input, and to provide automatic insertion of keywords, can reduce the number of careless constructs and hence reduce the number of complaints from *lint*.

But none of these will replace the need for programmers to know their language well, to think while they are coding, and to exercise care when writing programs in any language.

## NOTE

As this goes to press, there are two recent announcements that will affect the future of UNIX, but that I hope will not affect C very much: The AT&T/Sun "merged System V" and the opposing "Open" Software Foundation. If these two groups go ahead with their plans to produce two "competing standards," it will mean (apart from splintering the UNIX community just when there was danger of peace breaking out) continued portability problems of the same type as the USG/Berkeley differences that have been a thorn in everyone's side for years. However, it will not likely have much effect on the C language itself, and hence not much effect on *lint*.

# A

## The Ten Commandments for C Programmers

Henry Spencer* wrote these commandments based upon many years of debugging C code and thinking about the C language. The student of C is urged to reflect upon them, and act upon them.

1. Thou shalt run *lint* frequently and study its pronouncements with care, for verily its perception and judgement oft exceed thine.

---

* Commandments copyright © 1988 Henry Spencer, University of Toronto. Used by permission.

2. Thou shalt not follow the NULL pointer, for chaos and madness await thee at its end.

3. Thou shalt cast all function arguments to the expected type if they are not of that type already, even when thou art convinced that this is unnecessary, lest they take cruel vengeance upon thee when thou least expect it.

4. If thy header files fail to declare the return types of thy library functions, thou shalt declare them thyself with the most meticulous care, lest grievous harm befall thy program.

5. Thou shalt check the array bounds of all strings (indeed, all arrays), for surely where thou typest `foo` someone someday shall type `supercalifragilisticexpialidocious`.

6. If a function be advertised to return an error code in the event of difficulties, thou shalt check for that code, yea, even though the checks triple the size of thy code and produce aches in thy typing fingers, for if thou thinkest "it cannot happen to me," the gods shall surely punish thee for thy arrogance.

7. Thou shalt study thy libraries and strive not to re-invent them without cause, that thy code may be short and readable and thy days pleasant and productive.

8. Thou shalt make thy program's purpose and structure clear to thy fellow man by using the One True Brace Style*, even if thou likest it not, for thy creativity is better used in solving problems than in creating beautiful new impediments to understanding.

9. Thy external identifiers shall be unique in the first six characters, though this harsh discipline be irksome and the years of its necessity stretch before thee seemingly without end, lest thou tear thy hair out and go mad on that fateful day when thou desirest to make thy program run on an old system.

10. Thou shalt foreswear, renounce, and abjure the vile heresy which claimeth that "All the world's a VAX," and have no commerce with the benighted heathens who cling to this barbarous belief, that the days of thy program may be long even though the days of thy current machine be short.

---

* The One True Brace Style is the style of program layout demonstrated in [KeR78].

# B

## A Very Brief History of UNIX

Research
USG
Berkeley

The history of UNIX is complex enough to be the subject of an entire book. Here is a vastly over-simplified overview of the three main flavors of the system: Research, Berkeley, and USG.

## Research

"Research" is the Mt. Olympus of UNIX, AT&T Bell Laboratories Computer Science Research. Of the good folk who invented UNIX, Ken Thompson, Dennis Ritchie, Brian Kernighan, Doug McIlroy and several others still work at Research a decade and a half later. Research UNIXex have names like Seventh Edition, also called Version Seven, abbreviated V7. The current research version is Version Nine.

## USG

The USG was originally the UNIX Support Group, an organization formed within "the Bell System" (now AT&T), to provide a single supported version of the system internally. The USG no longer exists as such, but its name is commonly used to refer to this line of UNIX releases. USG releases of note include PWB (Programmer's Work-Bench, part of pre-history), System III, System V (abbreviated SV), System V Release 2 (SVR2), and System V Release 3 (SVR3, incorrectly abbreviated "3.0" by some AT&T staff). All System V releases are standardized by the *System V Interface Definition* [SVID2].

## Berkeley

Berkeley (The University of California at Berkeley) is home of many additions to UNIX: the first demand paging implementation for the DEC VAX, the C shell, the *vi* editor, the Berkeley implementation of TCP/IP, etc., as well as a large variety of software contributed by other universities, companies and individuals. Berkeley versions of UNIX are called BSD, for Berkeley Software Distribution. The most important releases are probably 4.2BSD and 4.3BSD.

Here is a *simplified* diagram of the historical relationships among the variants.

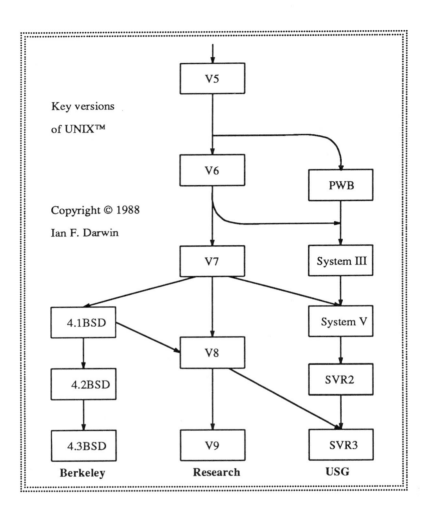

Key versions
of UNIX™

Copyright © 1988

Ian F. Darwin

# C

## Supplemental Programs

This section contains the man page for each of the programs mentioned in Chapter 5.

| Name | Function |
|------|----------|
| *clash* | Report long-name clashes |
| *cchk* | C checker; catches `if (a=b)` ... |
| *check* | Another C checker; catches `if (a=b)` ... |
| *printfck* | Lets *lint* check *printf*-like functions |
| *shortc* | Makes *cpp* work around long-name clashes |

Since most readers of this book are expected to be users of UNIX systems, or to have some access to UNIX systems, we have used the UNIX network as the primary distribution media for the source of these programs. The public domain programs discussed in this book are available free from UUNET (that is, free except for UUNET's usual connect-time charges). If you have access to UUNET, you can retrieve the source code using UUCP or FTP. These programs are stored in one compressed *tar* archive per program. The archives available are *check*, *cchk*, *clash*, *error*, *printfck*, and *shortc*. The syntax for getting the *check* program via UUCP, for example, is:

```
uucp uunet\!~/nutshell/lint/check.tar.Z yourhost\~/yourname/
```

The backslashes can be omitted if you use the Bourne shell (*sh*) instead of *csh*. The file should appear some time later (up to a day or more) in the lint */usr/spool/uucppublic/* **yourname**.

You don't need to subscribe to UUNET to be able to use their archives via UUCP. By calling 1-900-468-7727 and using the login "uucp" with no password, anyone may *uucp* any of UUNET's on line source collection. (Start by copying *uunet!~/ls-lR.Z*, which is a compressed index of every file in the archives.) As of this writing, the cost is 40 cents per minute. The charges will appear on your next telephone bill.

To use FTP, you will need to find a machine with direct access to the Internet. A sample session is shown, with commands in boldface.

```
% ftp uunet.uu.net
Name (uunet.uu.net:ambar): anonymous
Password: ambar@ora.com (use your user name and host here)
ftp> cd nutshell/lint
ftp> binary (you must specify binary transfer for compressed files)
ftp> get check.tar.Z
ftp> quit
%
```

The file is a compressed tar archive. To unpack it once you have retrieved the archive, type:

```
% uncompress check.tar.Z
% tar xf check.tar
```

System V systems require the following tar command instead:

```
% tar xof check.tar
```

Name

    clash – find indistinguishable or long identifiers

Synopsis

    **clash** [ **–actdsm***n* ] [ file ] . . .

Description

    *clash* finds identifiers that are not distinct in the first *numSigChars* characters, or finds identifiers that are longer than *numSigChars* characters. It lexically analyzes its input, ignoring comments. It does not parse, so it does not understand scoping. Some restrictions that *clash* might help detect:

–     Most UNIX file systems consider file names (components of pathnames) identical if their first 14 characters are identical.

–     Many UNIX assemblers and the loaders consider only the first eight characters of an identifier.

–     Many C compilers treat identifiers as identical if their first seven characters are the same (eight for identifiers that are not external). In fact, the ANSI C standard will probably make it legal for conforming compilers to ignore all but the first six characters and to ignore case distinctions.

–     *yacc* terminals become C preprocessor symbols, and should therefore differ within the first eight characters.

    The argument list is a sequence of input file names and flags. If no input file name is given, the standard input is processed.

    A flag operand starts with "–" and continues with any number of option names. Flags d, l, s, and m toggle a corresponding switch.

    *–a*    the input is a PDP-11 assembler program

    *–c*    the input is a C program (default)

    *–t*    the input is some other language ("text")

    *–d*    dump on error (this is useful for debugging *clash* itself)

    *–l*    print long identifiers

|     |     |
| --- | --- |
| −*s* | separate: process each file independently |
| −*m* | monocase: case distinctions don't count (the flag toggles the option which is initially off) |
| −*n* | sets *numSigChars* (default is 7) |

Local Info

> Written at the University of Toronto by D. Hugh Redelmeier.

Bugs

> Understands neither libraries nor #include commands: all relevant files must be explicitly scanned.
>
> The maximum number of distinct symbols and the maximum number of aggregate characters in them are fixed when *clash* is compiled.
>
> Does not understand Reiserisms: it presumes tokens are atomic in the macro-processing phase (this is a feature).

Name

    cchk – C program checker

Syntax

    **cchk** [ **–q** ] [ **–v** ] [ **–w** ] [ file ] ...

Description

cchk checks C programs for correctly matching brackets of all kinds (including quotes and comment brackets), checks that the indentation of matching brackets also matches, and checks for symptoms of three kinds of errors that the C compiler allows without warning: 'dangling else' errors where an else is bound to the wrong preceding if, nested comments (where the first close-comment bracket prematurely ends the outer comment), and the use of assignment ('=') where equality-test ('==') was meant. It is faster than the compiler and produces better messages; in particular, it localizes bracketing problems much more accurately.

The indentation rules it applies are that the indentation of the first non-white character on the line holding an opener should match that on the line holding the matching closer. These rules are fairly weak (e.g. they are compatible with but do not enforce various format standards), though they may still conflict with your own habits.

The –q (quiet) option suppresses messages classed as warnings, which includes those about mismatched indentations.

The –v (verbose) option prints more information — it shows what is on the internal stack at the time an error is detected. This is probably only of real use for debugging cchk itself.

The –w option suppresses non-zero exit statuses caused by warnings. This facilitates interface to *make*(1).

The distinction between warnings and errors is somewhat arbitrary. Because C allows certain errors, it would be inappropriate here to make the distinction between compilable and non-compilable programs. Basically only indentation mismatches are warnings, and the symptoms of dangling elses or using assignment ('=') instead of equality ('==') are treated as errors. The program will always print some message if you have an error involving mismatched brackets of some kind, and will pass any legal program if its indentation is also correct, unless '=' is used in the top level of a condition expression. For cases in between, it tries hard but may make mistakes, though if you are aiming for a properly indented program you can be sure that an error means that something is wrong.

When *cchk* detects signs of a bracket mismatch it makes a decision on the spot about the most likely underlying cause. It does not wait for more evidence to disambiguate this, so it sometimes gets confused. The summary it gives at the end tells you whether there was really a net imbalance of brackets, which may help sort out these cases.

See Also

*lint*(1), *cc*(1)

Diagnostics

*cchk* returns status 1 if warnings were issued, status 2 if errors were detected, and 0 if neither. The −*w* option changes the warnings-only exit status to 0.

History

Written by Steve Draper at Berkeley. Both the code and the manual page have been extensively cleaned up.

Bugs

When it gets confused, it can misdiagnose problems and produce multiple messages unnecessarily.

It does not deal with the preprocessor intelligently. Redefinitions of C syntax, macros containing dubious syntax, nested conditional compilation, and 'conditional compilation' of things that are not legal C, will all produce problems.

Name

>    check – a C program checker

Syntax

>    **check** [*C pre-processor options*] ... *file1* [*file2* ...]

Description

>    *check* attempts to find possible errors in C programs. It does
>    not duplicate or replace *lint*(1) but finds some constructs
>    about which *lint*(1) is silent. Among the things that are
>    detected are nested comments, unterminated comments,
>    assignments in conditional contexts, if statements with null
>    then and no else and potentially ambiguous else statements
>
>    For each such construct a warning is given, identifying the
>    source file and line number where it occurs. If multiple files
>    are being checked, the name of each file is printed as check-
>    ing starts.
>
>    All leading '−' options are assumed to be C preprocessor
>    directives, except that an argument '−−' ends the options and
>    is otherwise ignored. All following arguments are assumed
>    to be C source file names.

See Also

>    *cpp*(1), *lint*(1)

Bugs

>    *check* is not at all forgiving of simple syntax errors, such as
>    missing or extra punctuation.
>
>    The grammar (deliberately) does not accept all currently legal
>    C programs; some obsolescent or weird constructs are not
>    allowed. No attempt has yet been made to handle ANSI C.

Author

>    Nick Crossley, Computer Consoles Inc., 9801 Muirlands
>    Boulevard, Irvine CA 92718 (714) 458-7282 (email:
>    ... !uunet!ccicpg!nick)

Name

> printfck – lint pre-processor for printf checking

Syntax

> printfck < file.c >tmp.c; lint tmp.c

Description

> *printfck* enables *lint* to check the correspondence between the format specifications (such as %d, %ld, %s) in the argument list to printf-like functions (such as *printf*, *scanf* and their relatives) against the number and type of actual arguments. The program copies stdin to stdout, but adds a first line:

```
#include "procent.h"
```

> and replaces each call to a *printf*-like function (*printf*, *sprintf*, *fprintf*, and others you may care to add to its source) such as:

```
sprintf(buf, "A %20s%*d", s, m, n);
```

> by:

```
sprintf(buf, "A %20s%*d", procent_s(s), procent_d(m),
        procent_d(n));
```

> Now lint can do the checking with:

```
lint -options procent.c other_sources ...
```

Files

> procent.c, procent.h – files needed when linting the output.

History

> From: aeb@mcvax.UUCP (Andries Brouwer)
> Newsgroups: net.sources
> Subject: printfck.c - Check printf format strings
> Date-Received: Fri, 5-Apr-85 06:23:11 EST
> Reply-To: aeb@mcvax.UUCP (Andries Brouwer)
> Organization: CWI, Amsterdam
>
> Man page added by Ian Darwin, ian@darwin.uucp.

Bugs

> Andries Brouwer just wrote this as a quick hack to check the Hack & Quest sources. If someone wants to make this into

something generally useful the first thing to do is to make printfck read the list of functions to check from a file or from its arguments.

There are some minor problems with the interaction with preprocessor directives (e.g., parts of a printf statement between #ifdef's or #define's containing quotes).

Perhaps this should have been done with *lex.*

Name

> shortc – make preprocessor defines to map C flexnames into
> unique short names

Syntax

> shortc [–symlen] [–p] file . . . > Short.h

Description

> *shortc* reads one or more C files and checks them all for
> identifier names that are not unique in the first SYMLEN
> characters (SYMLEN defaults to seven since that is the most
> common length on old C compiler). The output should be
> redirected into a file called, say, *short.h*, which must then be
> included into each file (or into a common header file).

History

> From: jim@ism780.UUCP
> Newsgroups: net.sources
> Subject: shortc: C program to map flexnames into short identifiers
> Date: Sun, 11-Dec-83 23:04:00 EST
>
> This manual page added by Ian Darwin.

Bugs

> Since the symbols being redefined are ambiguous within
> SYMLEN characters (that was the problem in the first place),
> the files must be compiled using a flexnames version of cpp.
> If you lack even that, turn the output into a *sed* script and
> massage the source files. In this case, you may need to
> specify *–p* to parse preprocessor lines, but watch for things
> like include-file names.
>
> If using *cpp,* preprocessor symbols should be weeded out by
> hand; otherwise they will cause (innocuous) redefinition mes-
> sages.

# Bibliography

The UNIX programming text mentioned in the opening quotations is [KeP84]. The paper on programming style is [DaC85].

The history of the C compilers is outlined in [DaC84] and is discussed more fully in [Ros84] and [Kri86]. *pcc* and *lint* were designed by Steve Johnson, then at Bell Labs Computing Science Research. *lint* was first described in a Bell Laboratories CSTR (Technical Report) [Joh78].

> *lint* was originally written primarily to test the front end of PCC; I had done the front end work, but hadn't written the code generator yet, and wanted to make the program do SOMETHING so that I could see if it was at all sane. It took me a while to realize that other people might find it useful... [Johnson, personal correspondence, October, 1986.].

Both programs were part of Seventh Edition UNIX, and the CSTR was reprinted with the V7 Manuals. The program and its documentation have made their way into almost every UNIX since then. The non-SVID incremental linting was provided by David Harrison of the University of Toronto.

*clash* was written by Hugh Redelmeier at the University of Toronto; Hugh was until recently at HCR Inc. (formerly Human Computing Resources Inc). *shortc* appeared in USENET *net.sources* in 1983 and was reposted to *mod.sources* in 1986.

C++ was first described in [Str84]. An expanded and updated presentation appears in textbook form in [Str86].

The System V Interface Definition is [SVID2].

[DaC84]    I. F. Darwin and G. Collyer, The Evolution of UNIX from 1974 to the present, Part 1, *Microsystems 5*, 11 (November 1984), 44.

[DaC85]    I. F. Darwin and G. Collyer, Can't Happen, or /*NOTREACHED*/, or Real Programs Dump Core, *Proc. USENIX Winter Conference, Dallas TX,* January, 1985.

[dpANS]    Draft Proposed American National Standard for Information Systems—Programming Language C, X3J11 88-090, American National Standards Institute, May 13, 1988.

[Joh78]    S. C. Johnson, lint, a C Program Checker, *Computer Science Technical Report Number 65,* 1978.

[KeR78]    B. Kernighan and D. Ritchie, The C Programming Language, ISBN: 0-13-110163-3, 1978.

[KeP84]    B. Kernighan and R. Pike, The UNIX Programming Environment, ISBN: 0-13-937681-X, 1984.

[KeR88]    B. Kernighan and D. Ritchie, The C Programming Language, Second Edition, 1988.

[Kri86]    D. M. Kristol, Four Generations of the Portable C Compiler, *Proc. USENIX Summer Conference, Atlanta, GA,* June 1986.

[Ros84]   L. Rosler, The Evolution of C, *Bell Laboratories Technical Journal (BLTJ) 63* 8 (October 1984), 1685, AT&T Bell Laboratories.

[Str84]   B. Stroustrup, The C++ Reference Manual, *Computer Science Technical Report Number 108*, January 1, 1984.

[Str86]   B. Stroustrup, The C++ Programming Language, 1986.

[SVID2]   System V Interface Definition, Issue Two, ISBN: 0-932764-10-X, 1986.

Several people helped make this book what it is. Brian Kernighan made helpful comments on the structure of a very early draft. My University of Toronto students in CSC209H read —and sometimes made use of—an intermediate draft. Geoff Collyer of the University of Toronto made valuable technical comments on an early draft. Geoff also wrote with me the history paper from which Appendix B is derived. Mark Brader of SoftQuad waded through two complete drafts and, in effect, de*lint*ed the manuscript. Henry Spencer of the University of Toronto read a near-final draft, catching some technical problems, and re-wording several poorly-crafted phrases in the process. My wife Betty Cerar caught several stylistic abuses and numerous typographical and formatting errors. To all of them, and you, the reader, my thanks.

# Index

syntax-directed editors  49
System V Interface Definition
66

## T

trend toward more C-
compiler checking  2, 48
ttyin  10

## U

−*U* option
UNIX
  Eighth Edition (V8)   12
  history of  52
unsigned vs signed  21
USG  52

## V

−*v* option
<*varargs.h*>  12, 17
/*VARARGS*/ lint comment
12
void type  8

## X

−*x* option
X3J11  47

# UNIX

*From the best-selling* The Whole Internet *to our Nutshell Handbooks, there's something here for everyone. Whether you're a novice or expert UNIX user, these books will give you just what you're looking for: user-friendly, definitive information on a range of UNIX topics.*

## Using UNIX

### Connecting to the Internet: An O'Reilly Buyer's Guide  **NEW**

*By Susan Estrada*
*1st Edition August 1993*
*188 pages*
*ISBN 1-56592-061-9*

More and more people are interested in exploring the Internet, and this book is the fastest way for you to learn how to get started. This book provides practical advice on how to determine the level of Internet service right for you, and how to find a local access provider and evaluate the services they offer.

### !%@:: A Directory of Electronic Mail **NEW** Addressing & Networks

*By Donnalyn Frey & Rick Adams*
*3rd Edition August 1993*
*458 pages, ISBN 1-56592-031-7*

The only up-to-date directory that charts the networks that make up the Internet, provides contact names and addresses, and describes the services each network provides. It includes all of the major Internet-based networks, as well as various

commercial networks such as CompuServe, Delphi, and America Online that are "gatewayed" to the Internet for transfer of electronic mail and other services. If you are someone who wants to connect to the Internet, or someone who already is connected but wants concise, up-to-date information on many of the world's networks, check out this book.

### Learning the UNIX Operating System  **NEW**

*By Grace Todino, John Strang & Jerry Peek*
*3rd Edition August 1993*
*108 pages, ISBN 1-56592-060-0*

If you are new to UNIX, this concise introduction will tell you just what you need to get started and no more. Why wade through a six-hundred-page book when you can begin working productively in a matter of minutes? This book is the most effective introduction to UNIX in print. This new edition has been updated and expanded to provide increased coverage of window systems and networking. It's a handy book for someone just starting with UNIX, as well as someone who encounters a UNIX system as a visitor via remote login over the Internet.

## The Whole Internet User's Guide & Catalog

THE WHOLE INTERNET
USER'S GUIDE & CATALOG

By Ed Krol
1st Edition September 1992
400 pages, ISBN 1-56592-025-2

A comprehensive—and best-selling—introduction to the Internet, the international network that includes virtually every major computer site in the world. The Internet is a resource of almost unimaginable wealth. In addition to electronic mail and news services, thousands of public archives, databases, and other special services are available: everything from space flight announcements to ski reports. This book is a comprehensive introduction to what's available and how to find it. In addition to electronic mail, file transfer, remote login, and network news, *The Whole Internet* pays special attention to some new tools for helping you find information. Whether you're a researcher, a student, or just someone who likes electronic mail, this book will help you to explore what's possible.

## Smileys

By David W. Sanderson, 1st Edition March 1993
93 pages, ISBN 1-56592-041-4

Originally used to convey some kind of emotion in an e-mail message, smileys are some combination of typographic characters that depict sideways a happy or sad face. Now there are hundreds of variations, including smileys that depict presidents, animals, and cartoon characters. Not everyone likes to read mail messages littered with smileys, but almost everyone finds them humorous. The smileys in this book have been collected by David Sanderson, whom the *Wall Street Journal* called the "Noah Webster of Smileys."

## UNIX Power Tools

By Jerry Peek, Mike Loukides, Tim O'Reilly, et al.
1st Edition March 1993
1162 pages
(Bantam ISBN)
0-553-35402-7

Ideal for UNIX users who hunger for technical—yet accessible—information, *UNIX Power Tools* consists of tips, tricks, concepts, and freely-available software. Covers add-on utilities and how to take advantage of clever features in the most popular UNIX utilities. CD-ROM included.

## Learning the Korn Shell    NEW

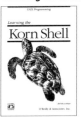

By Bill Rosenblatt
1st Edition June 1993
363 pages, ISBN 1-56592-054-6

This new Nutshell Handbook is a thorough introduction to the Korn shell, both as a user interface and as a programming language. Provides a clear explanation of the Korn shell's features, including *ksh* string operations, co-processes, signals and signal handling, and command-line interpretation. Also includes real-life programming examples and a Korn shell debugger (*kshdb*).

## Learning perl    NEW

By Randal L. Schwartz, 1st Edition November 1993 (est.)
220 pages (est.), ISBN 1-56592-042-2

Perl is rapidly becoming the "universal scripting language". Combining capabilities of the UNIX shell, the C programming language, *sed*, *awk*, and various other utilities, it has proved its use for tasks ranging from system administration to text processing and distributed computing. *Learning perl* is a step-by-step, hands-on tutorial designed to get you writing useful perl scripts as quickly as possible. In addition to countless code examples, there are numerous programming exercises, with full answers. For a comprehensive and detailed guide to programming with Perl, read O'Reilly's companion book *Programming perl*.

## Programming perl

By Larry Wall & Randal L. Schwartz
1st Edition January 1991, 428 pages, ISBN 0-937175-64-1

Authoritative guide to the hottest new UNIX utility in years, co-authored by its creator. Perl is a language for easily manipulating text, files, and processes.

## Learning GNU Emacs

By Deb Cameron & Bill Rosenblatt
1st Edition October 1991
442 pages, ISBN 0-937175-84-6

An introduction to the GNU Emacs editor, one of the most widely used and powerful editors available under UNIX. Provides a solid introduction to basic editing, a look at several important "editing modes" (special Emacs features for editing specific types of documents), and a brief introduction to customization and Emacs LISP programming. The book is aimed at new Emacs users, whether or not they are programmers.

## sed & awk

*By Dale Dougherty, 1st Edition November 1992*
*414 pages, ISBN 0-937175-59-5*

For people who create and modify text files, *sed* and *awk* are power tools for editing. Most of the things that you can do with these programs can be done interactively with a text editor. However, using *sed* and *awk* can save many hours of repetitive work in achieving the same result.

## MH & xmh: E-mail for Users & Programmers

*By Jerry Peek, 2nd Edition September 1992*
*728 pages, ISBN 1-56592-027-9*

Customize your e-mail environment to save time and make communicating more enjoyable. *MH & xmh: E-mail for Users & Programmers* explains how to use, customize, and program with the MH electronic mail commands available on virtually any UNIX system. The handbook also covers *xmh*, an X Window System client that runs MH programs. The new second edition has been updated for X Release 5 and MH 6.7.2. We've added a chapter on *mbook*, new sections explaining under-appreciated small commands and features, and more examples showing how to use MH to handle common situations.

## Learning the vi Editor

*By Linda Lamb, 5th Edition October 1990*
*192 pages, ISBN 0-937175-67-6*

A complete guide to text editing with *vi*, the editor available on nearly every UNIX system. Early chapters cover the basics; later chapters explain more advanced editing tools, such as *ex* commands and global search and replacement.

## UNIX in a Nutshell:
## For System V & Solaris 2.0

*By Daniel Gilly and the staff of O'Reilly & Associates*
*2nd Edition June 1992, 444 pages, ISBN 1-56592-001-5*

You may have seen UNIX quick reference guides, but you've never seen anything like *UNIX in a Nutshell*. Not a scaled-down quick-reference of common commands, *UNIX in a Nutshell* is a complete reference containing all commands and options, along with generous descriptions and examples that put the commands in context. For all but the thorniest UNIX problems this one reference should be all the documentation you need. Covers System V Releases 3 and 4 and Solaris 2.0.

An alternate version of this quick-reference is available for Berkeley UNIX.
*Berkeley Edition, December 1986*
*(latest update October 1990)*
*272 pages, ISBN 0-937175-20-X*

## Using UUCP and Usenet

*By Grace Todino & Dale Dougherty*
*1st Edition December 1986 (latest update October 1991)*
*210 pages, ISBN 0-937175-10-2*

Shows users how to communicate with both UNIX and non-UNIX systems using UUCP and *cu* or *tip*, and how to read news and post articles. This handbook assumes that UUCP is already running at your site.

# System Administration

## Managing UUCP and Usenet

*By Tim O'Reilly & Grace Todino*
*10th Edition January 1992*
*368 pages, ISBN 0-937175-93-5*

For all its widespread use, UUCP is one of the most difficult UNIX utilities to master. This book is for system administrators who want to install and manage UUCP and Usenet software. "Don't even TRY to install UUCP without it!"—Usenet message 456@nitrex.UUCP

## sendmail  **NEW**

*By Bryan Costales, with Eric Allman & Neil Rickert*
*1st Edition October 1993 (est.)*
*600 pages (est.), ISBN 0-937175-056-2*

This new Nutshell Handbook is far and away the most comprehensive book ever written on *sendmail*, a program that acts like a traffic cop in routing and delivering mail on UNIX-based networks. Although *sendmail* is the most widespread of all mail programs, it's also one of the last great uncharted territories—and most difficult utilities to learn—in UNIX system administration. The book covers both major versions of *sendmail*: the standard version available on most systems, and IDA *sendmail*, a version from Europe.

## termcap & terminfo

*By John Strang, Linda Mui & Tim O'Reilly*
*3rd Edition July 1992*
*270 pages, ISBN 0-937175-22-6*

For UNIX system administrators and programmers. This handbook provides information on writing and debugging terminal descriptions, as well as terminal initialization, for the two UNIX terminal databases.

## DNS and BIND

*By Cricket Liu & Paul Albitz, 1st Edition October 1992*
*418 pages, ISBN 1-56592-010-4*

*DNS and BIND* contains all you need to know about the Domain Name System (DNS) and BIND, its UNIX implementation. The Domain Name System (DNS) is the Internet's "phone book"; it's a database that tracks important information (in particular, names and addresses) for every computer on the Internet. If you're a system administrator, this book will show you how to set up and maintain the DNS software on your network.

## Essential System Administration

*By Æleen Frisch, 1st Edition October 1991*
*466 pages, ISBN 0-937175-80-3*

Provides a compact, manageable introduction to the tasks faced by everyone responsible for a UNIX system. This guide is for those who use a stand-alone UNIX system, those who routinely provide administrative support for a larger shared system, or those who want an understanding of basic administrative functions. Covers all major versions of UNIX.

## X Window System Administrator's Guide

*By Linda Mui & Eric Pearce*
*1st Edition October 1992*
*372 pages, With CD-ROM: ISBN 1-56592-052-X*
*Without CD-ROM: ISBN 0-937175-83-8*

This book is the first and only book devoted to the issues of system administration for X and X-based networks, written not just for UNIX system administrators but for anyone faced with the job of administering X (including those running X on stand-alone workstations). The *X Window System Administrator's Guide* is available either alone or packaged with the XCD. The CD provides X source code and binaries to complement the book's instructions for installing the software. It contains over 600 megabytes of X11 source code and binaries stored in ISO9660 and RockRidge formats. This will allow several types of UNIX workstations to mount the CD-ROM as a filesystem, browse through the source code and install pre-built software.

## Practical UNIX Security

*By Simson Garfinkel & Gene Spafford*
*1st Edition June 1991*
*512 pages, ISBN 0-937175-72-2*

Tells system administrators how to make their UNIX system—either System V or BSD—as secure as it possibly can be without going to trusted system technology. The book describes UNIX concepts and how they enforce security, tells how to defend against and handle security breaches, and explains network security (including UUCP, NFS, Kerberos, and firewall machines) in detail.

## Managing NFS and NIS

*By Hal Stern*
*1st Edition June 1991*
*436 pages, ISBN 0-937175-75-7*

*Managing NFS and NIS* is for system administrators who need to set up or manage a network filesystem installation. NFS (Network Filesystem) is probably running at any site that has two or more UNIX systems. NIS (Network Information System) is a distributed database used to manage a network of computers. The only practical book devoted entirely to these subjects, this guide is a must-have for anyone interested in UNIX networking.

## TCP/IP Network Administration

*By Craig Hunt*
*1st Edition July 1992*
*502 pages, ISBN 0-937175-82-X*

A complete guide to setting up and running a TCP/IP network for practicing system administrators. Covers how to set up your network, how to configure important network applications including *sendmail*, and discusses troubleshooting and security. Covers BSD and System V TCP/IP implementations.

## System Performance Tuning

*By Mike Loukides, 1st Edition November 1990*
*336 pages, ISBN 0-937175-60-9*

*System Performance Tuning* answers the fundamental question, "How can I get my computer to do more work without buying more hardware?" Some performance problems do require you to buy a bigger or faster computer, but many can be solved simply by making better use of the resources you already have.

## Computer Security Basics

*By Deborah Russell & G.T. Gangemi Sr.*
*1st Edition July 1991*
*464 pages, ISBN 0-937175-71-4*

Provides a broad introduction to the many areas of computer security and a detailed description of current security standards. This handbook describes complicated concepts like trusted systems, encryption, and mandatory access control in simple terms, and contains a thorough, readable introduction to the "Orange Book."

# UNIX Programming

## Understanding Japanese Information Processing `NEW`

*By Ken Lunde*
*1st Edition September 1993 (est.)*
*450 pages (est.), ISBN 1-56592-043-0*

*Understanding Japanese Information Processing* provides detailed information on all aspects of handling Japanese text on computer systems. It tries to bring all of the relevant information together in a single book. It covers everything from the origins of modern-day Japanese to the latest information on specific emerging computer encoding standards. There are over 15 appendices which provide additional reference material, such as a code conversion table, character set tables, mapping tables, an extensive list of software sources, a glossary, and much more.

## lex & yacc

*By John Levine, Tony Mason & Doug Brown*
*2nd Edition October 1992*
*366 pages, ISBN 1-56592-000-7*

Shows programmers how to use two UNIX utilities, *lex* and *yacc*, in program development. The second edition of *lex & yacc* contains completely revised tutorial sections for novice users and reference sections for advanced users. The new edition is twice the size of the original book, has an expanded index, and now covers Bison and Flex.

## High Performance Computing `NEW`

*By Kevin Dowd, 1st Edition June 1993*
*398 pages, ISBN 1-56592-032-5*

*High Performance Computing* makes sense of the newest generation of workstations for application programmers and purchasing managers. It covers everything, from the basics of modern workstation architecture, to structuring benchmarks, to squeezing more performance out of critical applications. It also explains what a good compiler can do—and what you have to do yourself. The book closes with a look at the high-performance future: parallel computers and the more "garden variety" shared memory processors that are appearing on people's desktops.

## ORACLE Performance Tuning `NEW`

*By Peter Corrigan & Mark Gurry*
*1st Edition September 1993 (est.)*
*650 pages (est.), ISBN 1-56592-048-1*

The ORACLE relational database management system is the most popular database system in use today. With more organizations downsizing and adopting client/server and distributed database approaches, system performance tuning has become vital. This book shows you the many things you can do to dramatically increase the performance of your existing ORACLE system. You may find that this book can save you the cost of a new machine; at the very least, it will save you a lot of headaches.

## POSIX Programmer's Guide

*By Donald Lewine, 1st Edition April 1991*
*640 pages, ISBN 0-937175-73-0*

Most UNIX systems today are POSIX-compliant because the Federal government requires it for its purchases. However, given the manufacturer's documentation, it can be difficult to distinguish system-specific features from those features defined by POSIX. The *POSIX Programmer's Guide*, intended as an explanation of the POSIX standard and as a reference for the POSIX.1 programming library, helps you write more portable programs.

## Understanding DCE

By Ward Rosenberry, David Kenney & Gerry Fisher
1st Edition October 1992
266 pages, ISBN 1-56592-005-8

A technical and conceptual overview of OSF's Distributed Computing Environment (DCE) for programmers and technical managers, marketing and sales people. Unlike many O'Reilly & Associates books, *Understanding DCE* has no hands-on programming elements. Instead, the book focuses on how DCE can be used to accomplish typical programming tasks and provides explanations to help the reader understand all the parts of DCE.

## Guide to Writing DCE Applications

By John Shirley
1st Edition July 1992
282 pages, ISBN 1-56592-004-X

A hands-on programming guide to OSF's Distributed Computing Environment (DCE) for first-time DCE application programmers. This book is designed to help new DCE users make the transition from conventional, nondistributed applications programming to distributed DCE programming. Covers the IDL and ACF files, essential RPC calls, binding methods and the name service, server initialization, memory management, and selected advanced topics. Includes practical programming examples.

## Power Programming with RPC

By John Bloomer
1st Edition February 1992
522 pages, ISBN 0-937175-77-3

RPC, or remote procedure calling, is the ability to distribute the execution of functions on remote computers. Written from a programmer's perspective, this book shows what you can do with RPC's, like Sun RPC, the de facto standard on UNIX systems. It covers related programming topics for Sun and other UNIX systems and teaches through examples.

## Managing Projects with make

By Andrew Oram & Steve Talbott
2nd Edition October 1991
152 pages, ISBN 0-937175-90-0

*make* is one of UNIX's greatest contributions to software development, and this book is the clearest description of *make* ever written. This revised second edition includes guidelines on meeting the needs of large projects.

## Software Portability with imake          NEW

By Paul DuBois
1st Edition July 1993
390 pages, 1-56592-055-4

*imake* is a utility that works with *make* to enable code to be complied and installed on different UNIX machines. This new Nutshell Handbook—the only book available on *imake*—is ideal for X and UNIX programmers who want their software to be portable. It includes a general explanation of *imake*, how to write and debug an *Imakefile*, and how to write configuration files. Several sample sets of configuration files are described and are available free over the Net.

## UNIX for FORTRAN Programmers

By Mike Loukides
1st Edition August 1990
264 pages, ISBN 0-937175-51-X

This book provides the serious scientific programmer with an introduction to the UNIX operating system and its tools. The intent of the book is to minimize the UNIX entry barrier and to familiarize readers with the most important tools so they can be productive as quickly as possible. *UNIX for FORTRAN Programmers* shows readers how to do things they're interested in: not just how to use a tool such as *make* or *rcs*, but how to use it in program development and how it fits into the toolset as a whole. "An excellent book describing the features of the UNIX FORTRAN compiler *f77* and related software. This book is extremely well written." — American Mathematical Monthly, February 1991

## Practical C Programming

By Steve Oualline
2nd Edition January 1993
396 pages, ISBN 1-56592-035-X

C programming is more than just getting the syntax right. Style and debugging also play a tremendous part in creating programs that run well. *Practical C Programming* teaches you not only the mechanics of programming, but also how to create programs that are easy to read, maintain, and debug. There are lots of introductory C books, but this is the Nutshell Handbook! In the second edition, programs now conform to ANSI C.

## Checking C Programs with lint

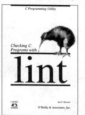

By Ian F. Darwin
1st Edition October 1988
84 pages, ISBN 0-937175-30-7

The *lint* program is one of the best tools for finding portability problems and certain types of coding errors in C programs. This handbook introduces you to *lint*, guides you through running it on your programs, and helps you interpret *lint's* output.

## Using C on the UNIX System

By Dave Curry
1st Edition January 1989
250 pages, ISBN 0-937175-23-4

*Using C on the UNIX System* provides a thorough introduction to the UNIX system call libraries. It is aimed at programmers who already know C but who want to take full advantage of the UNIX programming environment. If you want to learn how to work with the operating system and to write programs that can interact with directories, terminals, and networks at the lowest level you will find this book essential. It is impossible to write UNIX utilities of any sophistication without understanding the material in this book. "A gem of a book. The author's aim is to provide a guide to system programming, and he succeeds admirably. His balance is steady between System V and BSD-based systems, so readers come away knowing both." — SUN Expert, November 1989

## Guide to OSF/1

By the staff of O'Reilly & Associates
1st Edition June 1991
304 pages, ISBN 0-937175-78-1

This technically competent introduction to OSF/1 is based on OSF technical seminars. In addition to its description of OSF/1, it includes the differences between OSF/1 and System V Release 4 and a look ahead at DCE.

## Understanding and Using COFF

By Gintaras R. Gircys
1st Edition November 1988
196 pages, ISBN 0-937175-31-5

COFF—Common Object File Format—is the formal definition for the structure of machine code files in the UNIX System V environment. All machine-code files are COFF files. This handbook explains COFF data structure and its manipulation.

# *Career*

## Love Your Job! **NEW**

By Dr. Paul Powers, with Deborah Russell
1st Edition August 1993
210 pages, ISBN 1-56592-036-8

Do you love your job? Too few people do. In fact, surveys show that 80 to 95 percent of Americans are dissatisfied with their jobs. Considering that most of us will work nearly 100,000 hours during our lifetimes (half the waking hours of our entire adult lives!), it's sad that our work doesn't bring us the rewards—both financial and emotional—that we deserve. *Love Your Job!* is an inspirational guide to loving your work. It consists of a series of one-page reflections, anecdotes, and exercises aimed at helping readers think more deeply about what they want out of their jobs. Each can be read individually (anyplace, anytime, whenever you need to lift your spirits), or the book can be read and treated as a whole. *Love Your Job!* informs you, inspires you, and challenges you, not only to look outside at the world of work, but also to look inside yourself at what work means to you.

# O'Reilly Online Services

## How to Get Information about O'Reilly & Associates

The online O'Reilly Information Resource is a Gopher server that provides you with information on our books, how to download code examples, and how to order from us. There is also a UNIX bibliography you can use to get information on current books by subject area.

## Connecting to the O'Reilly Information Resource

Gopher is an interactive tool that organizes the resources found on the Internet as a sequence of menus. If you don't know how Gopher works, see the chapter "Tunneling through the Internet: Gopher" in *The Whole Internet User's Guide and Catalog* by Ed Krol.

An easy way to use Gopher is to download a Gopher client, either the tty Gopher that uses curses or the Xgopher.

Once you have a local Gopher client, you can launch Gopher with:

    gopher gopher.ora.com

To use the Xgopher client, enter:

    xgopher -xrm "xgopher.rootServer:
    gopher.ora.com"

If you have no client, log in on our machine via telnet and run Gopher from there, with:

    telnet gopher.ora.com
    login: gopher  (no password)

Another option is to use a World Wide Web browser, and enter the http address:

    gopher://gopher.ora.com

Once the connection is made, you should see a root menu similar to this:

```
Internet Gopher Information Client v1.12
    Root gopher server: gopher.ora.com

->1. News Flash! -- New Products and
     Projects of ORA/.
   2. About O'Reilly & Associates.
   3. Book Descriptions and Information/
   4. Complete Listing of Book Titles.
   5. FTP Archive and E-Mail Information/
   6. Ordering Information/
   7. UNIX Bibliography/

Press ? for Help, q to Quit, u to go up a
menu                        Page: 1/1
```

From the root menu you can begin exploring the information that we have available. If you don't know much about O'Reilly & Associates, choose About O'Reilly & Associates from the menu. You'll see an article by Tim O'Reilly that gives an overview of who we are—and a little background on the books we publish.

## Getting Information About Our Books

The Gopher server makes available online the same information that we provide in our print catalog, often in more detail.

Choose Complete Listing of Book Titles from the root menu to view a list of all our titles. This is a useful summary to have when you want to place an order.

To find out more about a particular book, choose Book Descriptions and Information; you will see the screen below:

```
Internet Gopher Information Client v1.12
    Book Descriptions and Information

->1. New Books and Editions/
   2. Computer Security/
   3. Distributed Computing Environment
     (DCE)/
   4. Non-Technical Books/
   5. System Administration/
   6. UNIX & C Programming/
   7. Using UNIX/
   8. X Resource/
   9. X Window System/
  10. CD-Rom Book Companions/
  11. Errata and Updates/
  12. Keyword Search on all Book
     Descriptions <?>
  13. Keyword Search on all Tables of
     Content <?>
```

All of our new books are listed in a single category. The rest of our books are grouped by subject. Select a subject to see a list of book titles in that category. When you select a specific book, you'll find a full description and table of contents.

For example, if you wanted to look at what books we had on administration, you would choose selection 5, System Administration, resulting in the following screen:

```
            System Administration

   1. DNS and BIND/
   2. Essential System Administration/
   3. Managing NFS and NIS/
   4. Managing UUCP and Usenet/
   5. sendmail/
   6. System Performance Tuning/
   7. TCP/IP Network Administration/
```

If you then choose `Essential System Administration`, you will be given the choice of looking at either the book description or the table of contents.

```
        Essential System Administration

->1.Book Description and Information.
  2.Book Table of Contents.
```

Selecting either of these options will display the contents of a file. Gopher then provides instructions for you to navigate elsewhere or quit the program.

### Searching For the Book You Want

Gopher also allows you to locate book descriptions or tables of contents by using a word search. (We have compiled a full-text index WAIS.)

If you choose `Book Descriptions and Information` from the root menu, the last two selections on that menu allow you to do keyword searches.

Choose `Keyword Search on all Book Descriptions` and you will be prompted with:

`Index word(s) to search for:`

Once you enter a keyword, the server returns a list of the book descriptions that match the keyword. For example, if you enter the keyword DCE, you will see:

```
Keyword Search on all Book Descriptions:
                   DCE

-> 1.Understanding DCE.
   2.Guide to Writing DCE Applications.
   3.Distributed Applications Across DCE
     and Windows NT.
   4.DCE Administration Guide.
   5.Power Programming with RPC.
   6.Guide to OSF/1.
```

Choose one of these selections to view the book description.

Using the keyword search option can be a faster and less tedious way to locate a book than moving through a lot of menus.

You can also use a WAIS client to access the full-text index or book descriptions. The name of the database is

`O'Reilly_Book_Descriptions.src`

and you can find it in the WAIS directory of servers.

**Note:** We are always adding functions and listings to the O'Reilly Information Resource. By the time you read this article, the actual screens may very well have changed.

### E-mail Accounts

E-mail ordering promises to be quick and easy, even faster than using our 800 number. Because we don't want you to send credit card information over a non-secure network, we ask that you set up an account with us in advance. To do so, either call us at 1-800-998-9938 or use the application provided in `Ordering Information` on the Gopher root menu. You will then be provided with a confidential account number.

Your account number allows us to retrieve your billing information when you place an order by e-mail, so you only need to send us your account number and what you want to order.

For your security, we use the credit card information and shipping address that we have on file. We also verify that the name of the person sending us the e-mail order matches the name on the account. If any of this information needs to change, we ask that you contact order@ora.com or call our Customer Service department.

### Ordering by E-mail

Once you have an account with us, you can send us your orders by e-mail. Remember that you can use our online catalog to find out more about the books you want. Here's what we need when you send us an order:

1. Address your e-mail to: order@ora.com
2. Include in your message:
   - The title of each book you want to order (including ISBN number, if you know it)
   - The quantity of each book
   - Method of delivery: UPS Standard, Fed Ex Priority...
   - Your name and account number
   - Anything special you'd like to tell us about the order

When we receive your e-mail message, our Customer Service representative will verify your order before we ship it, and give you a total cost. If you would like to change your order after confirmation, or if there are ever any problems, please use the phone and give us a call—e-mail has its limitations.

This program is an experiment for us. We appreciate getting your feedback so we can continue improving our service.

# O'Reilly & Associates Inc.
103A Morris Street, Sebastopol, CA 95472

**(800) 998-9938 • (707) 829-0515 • FAX (707) 829-0104 • order@ora.com**

## How to get information about O'Reilly books online

• If you have a local gopher client, then you can launch gopher and connect to our server:
`gopher gopher.ora.com`

• If you want to use the Xgopher client, then enter:
`xgopher -xrm "xgopher.rootServer: gopher.ora.com"`

• If you want to use telnet, then enter:
`telnet gopher.ora.com login: gopher [no password]`

• If you use a World Wide Web browser, you can access the gopher server
by typing the following http address:
`gopher://gopher.ora.com`

---

## WE'D LIKE TO HEAR FROM YOU

Which O'Reilly book did this card come from?

Is your job: ☐ SysAdmin? ☐ Programmer?

☐ Other? What?

Do you use other computer systems besides UNIX? If so, which one(s)?

Please send me the following:

☐ A free catalog of titles

☐ A list of bookstores in my area that carry O'Reilly books

☐ A list of distributors outside of the U.S. and Canada

☐ Information about bundling O'Reilly books with my product

Company Name

Name

Address

City/State

Zip/Country

Telephone

FAX

*Internet* or *Uunet* e-mail address

# O'Reilly & Associates Inc.

*(800) 998-9938* • *(707) 829-0515* • *FAX (707) 829-0104* • order@ora.com

**How to order books by e-mail:**

1. Address your e-mail to: order@ora.com
2. Include in your message:
   - The title of each book you want to order
     *(an ISBN number is helpful but not necessary)*
   - The quantity of each book
   - Your account number and name
   - Anything special you'd like us to know about your order

O'Reilly Online Account Number

Use our online catalog to find out more about our books (see reverse).

NO POSTAGE
NECESSARY IF
MAILED IN THE
UNITED STATES

# BUSINESS REPLY MAIL

FIRST CLASS MAIL   PERMIT NO. 80   SEBASTOPOL, CA

*Postage will be paid by addressee*

*O'Reilly & Associates, Inc.*

103A Morris Street

Sebastopol, CA  95472-9902